Learn Skills to Sew

like a professional

Practical tailoring methods and techniques

Naoko Domeki
Shihoko Makino

The standard professional techniques used in the process of
making clothing with a sewing machine are without a doubt doable,
no matter who does the sewing.
We will give you an introduction to how professionals
leave out steps to save time or take extra steps for a smarter finish.
Rather than using a machine designed for professionals,
we will use one that can be found in the average household,
to show the methods for sewing.
We will also provide a large number of photos presenting points for
smarter tailoring using professional sewing and ironing methods.
We hope this book will be a good reference for you
as you try out these techniques.

Reference Japanese Books: *Otoko no Shirts no Hon (The Book of Men's Shirts)*,
Sekai de Aisareru Print no Dress (The World's Most-Loved Print Dresses),
Rintoshita Otona no Fuku (Dignified Clothes for Adults), and *Karoyakana Otona no Fuku
(Easygoing Clothing for Adults)*

Tools

Sewing machine and attachments

●Presser feet

The sewing machine comes equipped with a presser foot that is suitable for most tasks. It is also important to use a presser foot most suitable for the sewing method so that the best finish can be achieved. Specific presser feet are sold separately as attachments for the sewing machine, and there are many specialized kinds. The presser feet introduced here are for use with the household zigzag sewing machine shown in the picture. There are also other varieties of presser feet, and the presser foot that is equipped differs depending on the machine type.

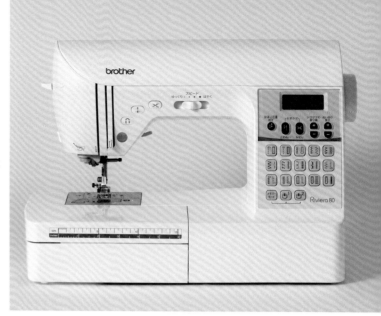

Zigzag foot
Standard presser foot. Used for straight-line sewing and zigzag sewing.

Straight stitch foot
Presser foot specialized for sewing straight lines. →p. 22

Rolled hem foot
Presser foot for creating a clean double hem at the edge of the fabric. →p. 23

Overlock foot
Presser foot for handling cut edges. →p. 22

Side cutter foot
Presser foot that creates a hem by cutting and sewing the edge of the fabric at the same time. →p. 26

Buttonhole foot
Presser foot for creating buttonholes. →p. 27

Gathering foot
Presser foot for doing stitching while tucking. →p. 26

Concealed zipper foot
Presser foot used for attaching invisible zippers. →p. 67

One-side zipper foot
Presser foot for using with normal zippers. →pp. 70, 73

Non stick foot
Presser foot for material that does not glide smoothly, such as leather and vinyl fabrics.

●Foot controller

The starting, stopping, and speed of the sewing machine can be controlled with this foot pedal. This is an attachment that you'll definitely want to have for speedy and beautiful sewing that can be done flexibly using both hands from start to finish.

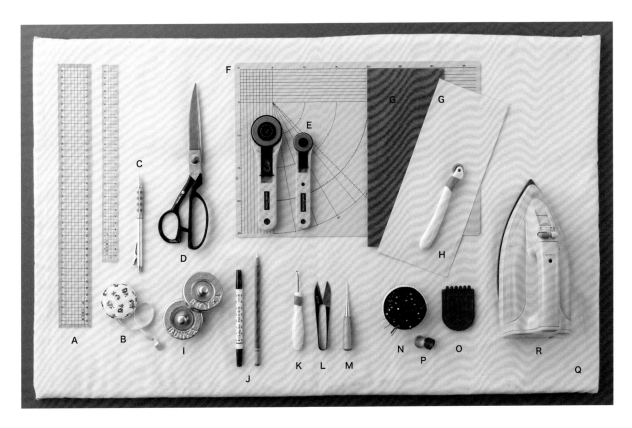

Handy presser feet available on the general market

These presser feet are set onto the needle bar of the sewing machine. Be sure to check before purchasing since some types may not fit your sewing machine.

Concealed zipper foot
Presser foot for concealing zippers.

2 mm presser foot
With a narrow width (2 mm), this presser foot is for adding a patch pocket, or sewing a front edge, or collar stitches when it is difficult to use a standard width presser foot.

Presser foot specialized for thin material
Presser foot with a small hole for the falling needle. The small hole means thin fabric that can be easily caught is neatly sewn.

Non stick foot
Presser foot for fabric that tends to stick such as leather or PVC.

Other tools

A Graph ruler

B Measuring tape

C Mechanical pencil

D Sewing scissors

E Rotary cutter

F Cutting board

G Double-sided tracing paper

H Roulette

I Weights

J Ink pen for fabric / chalk pencil

K Seam ripper

L Thread scissors

M Awl

N Pin cushion / marking pins

O Hand sewing needles

P Thimble

Q Ironing mat

R Steam iron

Fabric, thread, and needles

For sewing machine thread, the higher the number the thinner the thread; whereas for sewing machine needles, the higher the number the thicker the needle.

As a standard, fine threads and needles are used for thin fabrics, whereas thicker threads and needles are used for thick fabric.

For clothing, Shappe Span threads No. 60 and No. 90 are used, and needles No. 9 and No. 11 are often used. Thread No. 30 and needle No. 14 are used when you want the stitching to stand out on thicker fabrics.

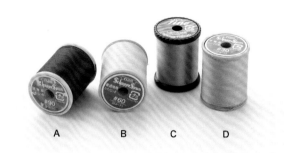

Sewing machine thread

A Shappe Span No. 90 (Polyester sewing machine thread)
B Shappe Span No. 60 (Polyester sewing machine thread)
C Fine (Polyester silk-type sewing machine thread)
D Shappe Span No. 30 (Polyester sewing machine thread)

Sewing machine needles

A No. 9
B No. 11
C No. 14

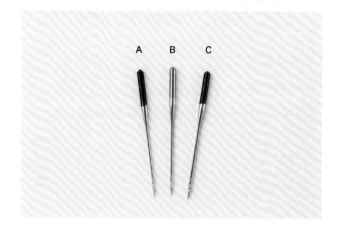

Chiffon georgette
Thin, supple fabric
Thread: Shappe Span No. 90
Needle: No. 9

Cotton lawn
Thin cotton
Thread: Shappe Span No. 90
Needle: No. 9

Silk taffeta
Thin fabric with tension
a Thread: Shappe Span No. 90, Needle: No. 9
b Thread: Fine, Needle: No. 9

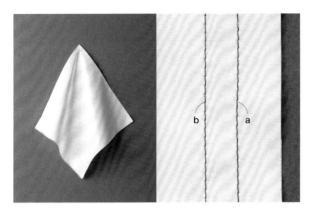

Cotton broadcloth
General cotton
a Thread: Shappe Span No. 60, Needle: No. 11
b Thread: Shappe Span No. 90, Needle: No. 9

Wool georgette
General wool
Thread: Shappe Span No. 60
Needle: No. 11

Cotton gabardine
Slightly thick cotton
Thread: Shappe Span No. 60
Needle: No. 11

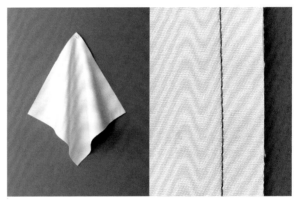

Thick denim
Thick cotton
Thread: Shappe Span No. 60
Needle: No. 11

Brushed wool
Thick wool
Thread: Shappe Span No. 60
Needle: No. 11

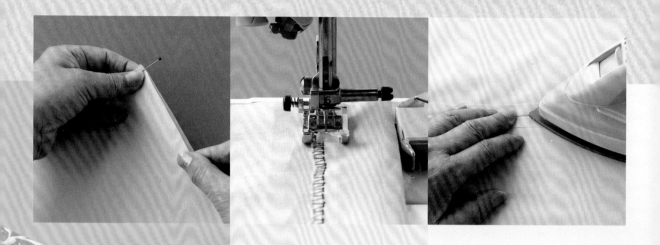

STANDARD
TECHNIQUES

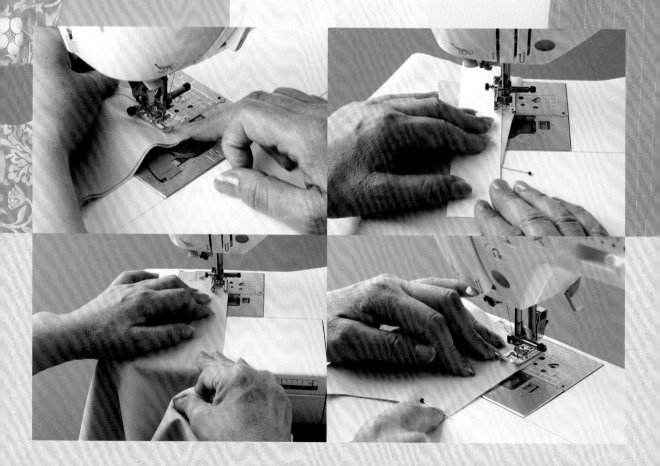

Joining two pieces of fabric

1 Place the two pieces of fabric together with right sides facing and first align the top edges, then match up the notch marks.

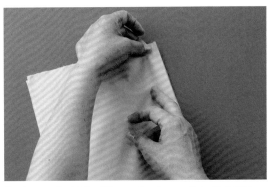

2 Arrange the fabric while pressing down on the upper edge. Use your other hand to straighten out any creases and align the pieces correctly.

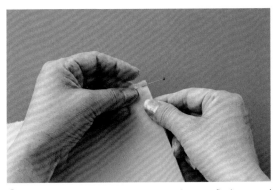

3 Place a marking pin where the upper edges are firmly pressed down. Fasten the pin at a right angle to the fabric edge.

4 Place your index finger in between the edges of the pieces and align them as far as the notch mark.

5 Fasten at the notch mark with a marking pin.

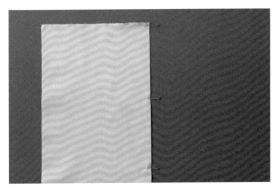

6 Flatten the fabric and fasten with a marking pin in the middle.

Sewing with the machine

Before you begin sewing, be absolutely sure to try sewing using a scrap piece from the fabric to be sewn to confirm thread tension.

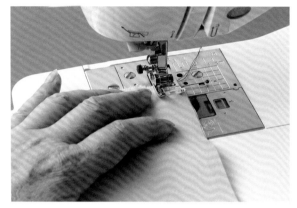

1 Place the fabric edge on the scale of the sewing machine's needle and lower the presser foot to hold the upper edge in place.

2 Remove the marking pin from the upper edge and sew three to four stitches using reverse stitching.

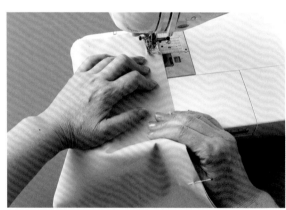

3 Slightly open the fingers of your left hand and firmly press down to prevent the fabric from shifting. With your right hand, hold the fabric as shown in the picture. Keep the position of the fabric pieces flat and gently pull the bottom of the fabric as you sew.

4 When you have sewn about 10 cm, take hold of stitched fabric with your left hand. Lightly pull it up and down to prevent puckering as you sew. Stitch to the marking pin, remove it, then continue sewing.

5 Press down on the edge of the fabric until the end for stitching, then finish by doing reverse stitching over the completed stitching.

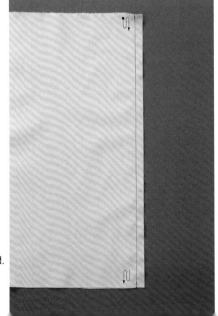

6 Completed.

Sewing thin fabric

With thin fabrics such as cotton lawn and chiffon georgette, the edges of the fabric easily catch in the machine as you start and finish stitching. Using thin paper, such as kraft paper or tracing paper, can help as you sew. Smooth sewing is accomplished using a presser foot with a small needle hole (**Straight stitch foot**→p. 4, **Presser foot specialized for thin material**→p. 5).

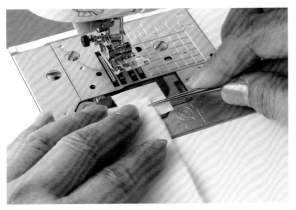 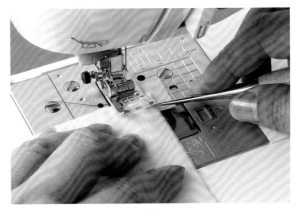

1 Use an awl to press a 3–4 cm piece of paper under the upper edge of the fabric as you begin reverse stitching.

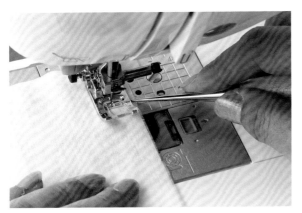 

2 Because thin fabric is likely to snag, sewing is done while the seam allowance is pressed with an awl.

3 Paper is also inserted underneath the fabric after sewing, and then reverse stitched.

5 Tear off the paper carefully at the top and bottom.

4 Completed piece with paper attached at the beginning and end of sewing.

Sewing fabric without marking pins

To save time, the two pieces can be directly sewn together on the machine without using marking pins.

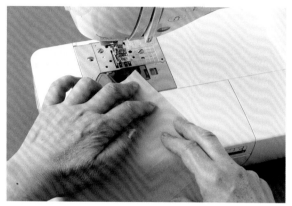

1   The two pieces are placed together wrong side out and put on the sewing machine. Place their upper edges under the presser foot.

2   Lower the presser foot, make 3–4 reverse stitches, to fix them in place at the top edge, and then leave the needle down, going through the fabric.

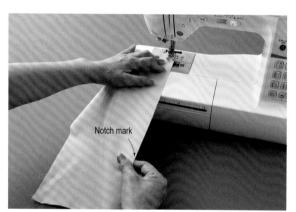

Notch mark

3   Line up the edges of the two fabric pieces and align the notch marks, holding firmly in place at that point.

4   Press the fabric as shown in the picture to fold it while holding it at the notch marks to keep the stitching position straight while sewing.

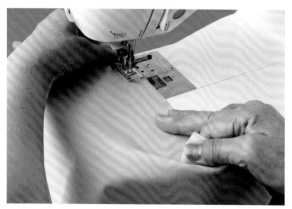

5   Once you have sewn 10 cm, take the stitched part in your left hand and pull tight as you keep sewing. Repeat 3 and 4 until the sewing is complete.

Sewing with a specified seam allowance

Instead of making finishing line marks, sew at the determined seam allowance width.

Using the needle plate scale as a guide

The scale of the needle plate dimensions is based on the needle's position, so sewing is done while aligning the fabric edges on the seam allowance scale.

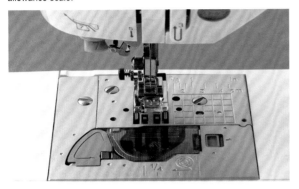

Using a stitch ruler

The magnetic stitch ruler is used by fixing it to the needle plate. Stitch rulers that are set on the needle bar may not be compatible with some sewing machines, so please check when purchasing.

Magnet type

Needle bar type

How to use a magnetic stitch ruler

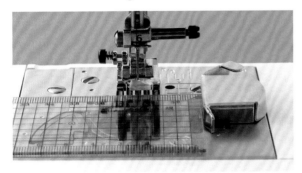

1   Measure the dimensions based on the location of the needle using a ruler, and fix the stitch ruler in place on the needle plate.

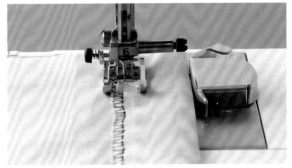

2   The edge of the fabric is held against the guide on the stitch ruler while sewing.

Using the width of the presser foot as a guide

When neither the needle plate scale nor the magnetic stitch ruler can be used, such as when stitching on a panel cut line, sewing is done using the presser foot as a width guide.

Preparing the seam allowance using an iron

When the sewing is finished, iron the seam. By pressing the stitching, it gives a smart finish to the seams.

Opening

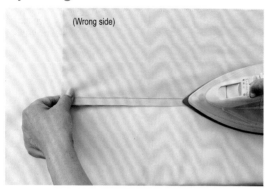

1   While the fabric is wrong side out, pull the ends of the fabric, and lightly steam-iron along the seam while pulling the edge of the fabric to stretch the seam tightly.

2   Use your fingers to open the seam allowance as you iron.

Using thick wool

Thick wool is difficult to iron effectively and bunches up if the seam allowance has a narrow opening, so cut with a seam allowance of a minimum of 1.2 cm, or if possible, 1.5 cm.

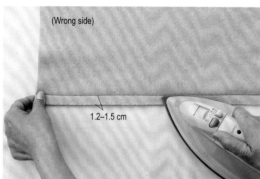

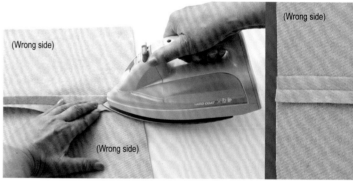

1   Turn the fabric wrong side out and iron on the seam. Be sure that steam iron is very lightly applied to the stitching so that an iron imprint isn't left. Firmly press down to flatten the seam allowance.

2   Press the stitching with the front edge of the iron while opening the seam allowance with your fingers. To make sure that an imprint of the seam allowance isn't left, and to make sure the texture of the fabric isn't lost, do not apply the whole iron to the seam allowance. Instead, tilt the iron forward and only apply the front edge.

Folding to one side

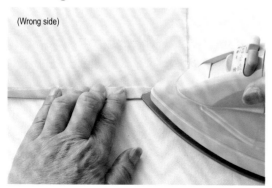

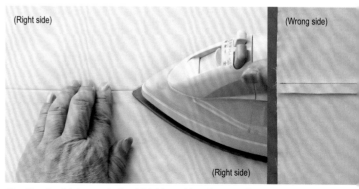

1   In the same way as with opening, iron lightly along the stitching. Bring the two seam allowances together from the stitching in the direction of the fold, apply the steam iron.

2   Turn the fabric over to the right side and iron the seam from the front.

Handling the seam allowance

The four commonly used methods are: opening, folding to one side, French seam, and flat-felled seam.
The method used will depend on the design and the fabric.

Opening the seam allowance

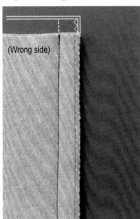

(Wrong side)

1 Overcast stitch or zigzag stitch (→p. 22) along the seam allowance edges then sew with the two fabrics turned wrong side out.

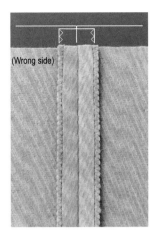

(Wrong side)

2 Open and neaten the seam allowance with an iron (→p. 14).

Zigzag stitching along the cut edge

● For the seam allowance, zigzag stitching is applied to the cut edge of the fabric, with the sewing done so that the needle falls on the cut edge.
● When opening the seam allowance, zigzag stitch from the right side of the fabric.
● When zigzag stitching on the cut edge of one piece of thin fabric, the fabric can bunch up at the edge, creating a poor finish.
   When that happens:
   ① Cut more of the seam allowance by 0.3–0.5 cm.
   ② Apply spray starch for ironing on the fabric edge and iron to keep the edge stiff.
   ③ Zigzag stitch 0.3–0.5 cm in from the fabric edge.
   ④ Be careful not to cut the sewing thread; instead, cut the fabric from the zigzag stitching.

When using thin fabrics

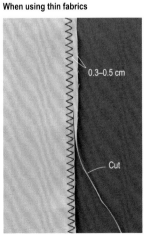

Apply to the cut edge

0.3–0.5 cm

Cut

Spray starch for ironing

Folding the seam allowance to one side...not for thick fabrics

(Wrong side)

Overcast stitch the two pieces together

(Wrong side)

1 The two pieces of fabric are stitched while wrong side out. Move the piece of fabric with the folded seam allowance to the bottom for sewing. Next, overcast stitch or zigzag stitch (→p. 22) the two pieces together on the edge of the seam allowance.

2 Fold and neaten the seam allowance on one side with an iron (→p. 14).

French seam ...for thin through normal fabrics

(Right side)

Just under half the seam allowance

(Right side)

1 Cut the fabric with a 1.5–2 cm seam allowance, and with the fabric right side out, sew the seam allowance about halfway in from the edge.

2 Open the seam allowance in step **1** with an iron.

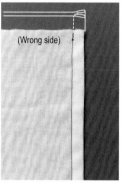

(Wrong side)

(Wrong side)

3 Fold the fabric wrong side out at the seam and sew the finishing line.

4 Fold the seam allowance on one side and then iron to neaten.→p. 14

Flat-felled seam...for thin through slightly thick fabric

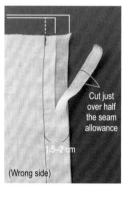

Cut just over half the seam allowance

1.5–2 cm

(Wrong side)

1 Cut the fabric with a seam allowance of 1.5–2 cm, and sew the two pieces of fabric wrong side out. When stitching, move the fabric with the folded seam allowance to the bottom for sewing. Next, cut off a bit more than half of the seam allowance from the side with the folded seam allowance.

(Wrong side)

(Wrong side)

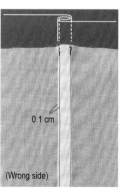

0.1 cm

(Wrong side)

(Right side)

2 Fold so that the narrow section of the seam allowance can wrap around the wide seam allowance.

3 Iron the two seam allowances in step **2** and fold.

4 Open the bottom piece of fabric and stitch the folds created in step **2** in each seam allowance.

5 From the right side, only one stitch is visible.

Dart sewing

Mark the dart position with an awl and sew. For fabric that is hard to mark with an awl, like wool (→p. 19), make tailor tacks.

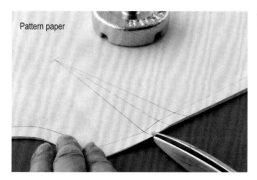

1 Lay the pattern paper on top of the cut fabric and cut slits at three places in the seam allowance edge where the darts are positioned (notch marks showing to cut in by 0.3 cm).

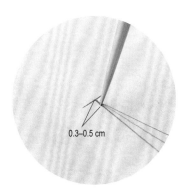

2 Perforate the tip of the darts to 0.3–0.5 cm in front with an awl and make a mark on the fabric.

3 Next, on the centerline of the dart section, add two or three marks with an awl.

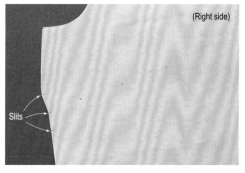

4 The finished marking.

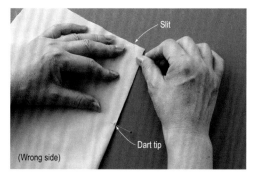

5 Turn the dart section wrong side out and line up the slits. Fasten the tip of the dart (0.3–0.5 cm from the mark made with an awl) with a marking pin, using a fingernail to mark the fold.

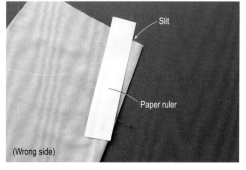

6 Using paper about as thick as a postcard, create a paper ruler that is longer than the length of the dart, lining it up with the slits and the dart tip.

 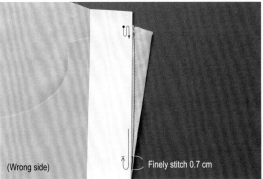

(Wrong side)   Finely stitch 0.7 cm

7 Take the ruler and sew the dart going from the slits to the tip. When beginning to reverse stitch, stitch at a slight angle as shown in the picture. For the front of the dart, finely stitch with a 0.7 cm needle, then reverse stitch.

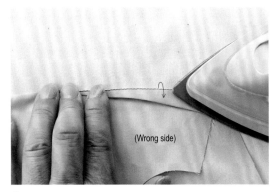 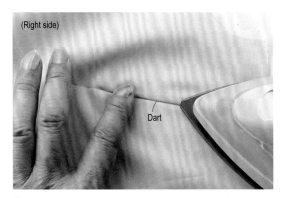

(Wrong side)

(Right side)

Dart

8 Apply an iron after folding the dart seam allowance from the stitch. Once folding is done in this manner using the iron, the seam will be completely finished.

9 Neaten the dart seam with an iron from the right side.

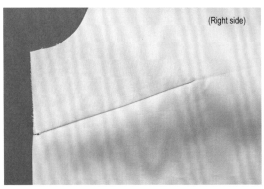 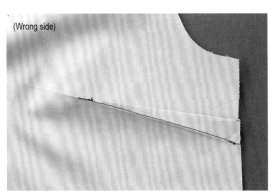

(Right side)   (Wrong side)

10 The sewn dart.

Marking thick fabrics...wool, etc.

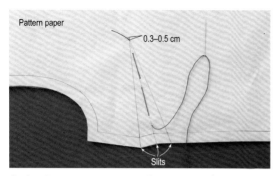

1 Lay the pattern paper on top of the cut fabric. Cut slits at the end of where the dart is positioned. Next, roughly sew the center of the dart using basting thread.

2 Cut the center of the roughly sewn thread.

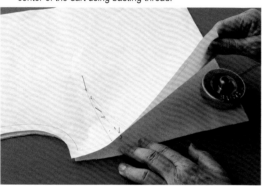

3 Remove the pattern paper carefully so that the thread doesn't come out.

4 Carefully fold back the top fabric and cut the center thread.

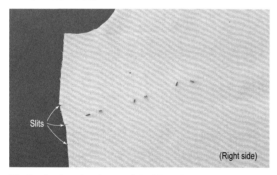

5 Cut the thread at the top of the fabric short to complete the marking.

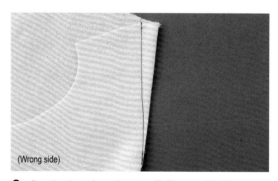

6 Sew the dart referencing steps 5–7 on pp. 17–18.

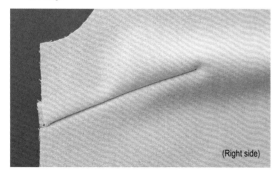

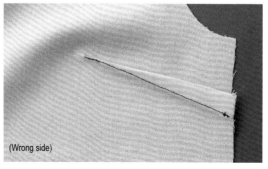

7 Arrange with an iron referencing steps 8–9 on p. 18.

Fitting the shoulders

How to add ease to the back shoulder when sewing. Sew with the eased back bodice on the bottom.

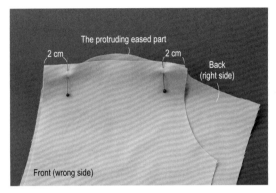

1 Turn the front part and the back part wrong side out. Flatten 2 cm sections at both ends and fasten with marking pins. The back shoulder will have surplus gathering that protrudes out.

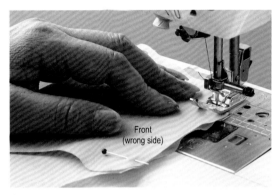

2 With the front bodice on top, place on the sewing machine, and sew from the edge of the fabric at the top to the marking pin.

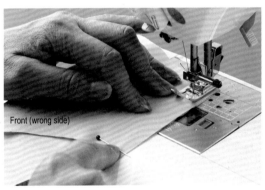

3 Pull the fabric slightly at the position of the lower marking pin to stretch the shoulder of the front bodice, and align the two pieces flat.

4 While lightly pulling the two aligned pieces, sew to the lower marking pin position.

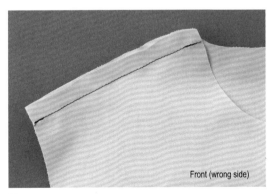

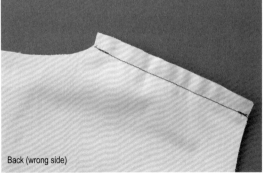

5 Sew the remaining portion at the end of the fabric. The ease has been sewn in at the back.

SEWING USING VARIOUS PRESSER FEET

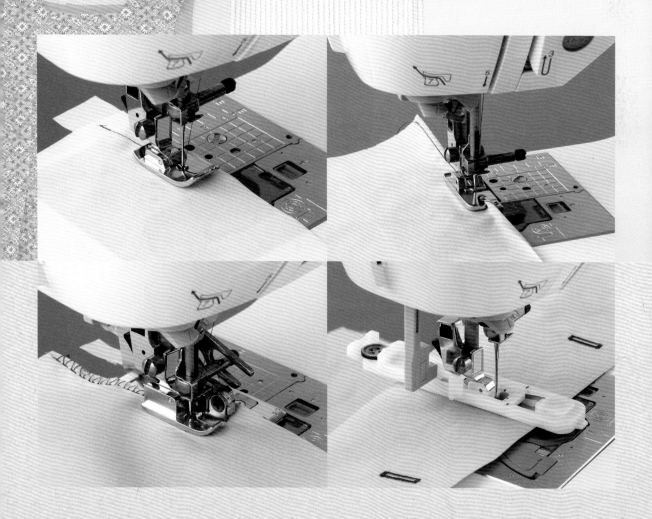

Straight stitch foot

- Presser foot specialized for sewing straight lines. In particular, you can cleanly sew thin fabric.
- The standard presser foot of a household sewing machine is also for zigzag stitching, it has a wide hole for the needle to drop. The straight stitch foot has a smaller hole, holding the fabric in place to where the needle drops, so the fabric doesn't get pulled up. This also prevents the seam puckering, even with thin fabric.
- When sewing thin fabrics, it is a good idea to attach paper (such as kraft paper or tracing paper) at the beginning and the end (→p. 11).

Straight stitch foot   Zigzag foot

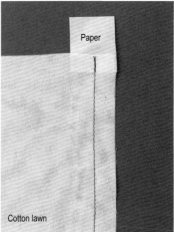

Paper

Cotton lawn

Overlock foot

- Presser foot for sewing overcast stitching to the edge of the fabric. The presser foot is used as a guide when sewing the edge, so it creates clean stitches. It can be used when handling cut edges with zigzag stitching.
- Sew from the right side of the fabric when you are working on one piece of fabric.
- When using thin fabrics like cotton lawn, sew the two pieces together, then overcast stitch on the combined ends and fold over to one side.

Wool georgette

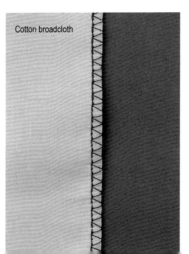

Cotton broadcloth

Cotton lawn

Overcast stitch the two pieces together

Rolled hem foot

●Use for finishing the hem. Presser foot for sewing while tightly double folding the ends of the fabric. Suitable for thin through to thick fabric.

Sewing in a straight line...fabric: cotton broadcloth

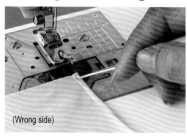

(Wrong side)

1 Finely double fold the edge of the fabric (0.3–0.5 cm), pushing the top end with an awl so it goes under the presser foot.

2 Bring down the presser foot and drop the needle on to the top end of the fabric.

3 Keep the needle dropped and raise the presser foot, then use an awl to wrap the fabric around the curled part of the presser foot.

(Wrong side)

4 Lower the presser foot and begin reverse stitching. As you fold the fabric edge about 0.5 cm with your right hand, use your left finger to create a standing fold in front of the foot, then sew while wrapping around the curled part of the foot.

5 The completed hem.

Sewing thin fabrics...fabric: chiffon georgette

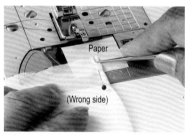

Paper

(Wrong side)

1 Finely double fold the fabric edge (0.3–0.5 cm) and fasten the top end with a marking pin. Place paper underneath the fabric (such as kraft paper or tracing paper) by pushing it under the presser foot with an awl.

2 Remove the marking pin and sew as you would in steps 2–4 above for Sewing in a straight line.

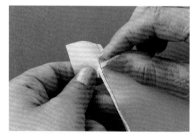

Loose stitches

3 Attach paper at the end of sewing as you did at the beginning, sew in place, then tear it out when sewing is complete.

4 The completed hem. Pay attention while sewing thin fabrics as the fabric may not fold in and can create loose stitches.

Sewing a curve...fabric: cotton broadcloth

Curves can cause the fabric edges to slip out of the fold and create loose stitches; by first staystitching the edge, then sewing a rolled hem, it creates a clean finish. This is also recommended for straight lines when the stitches come loose and you can't achieve a complete fold.

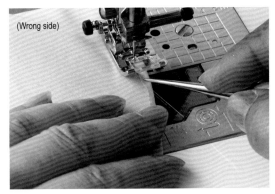

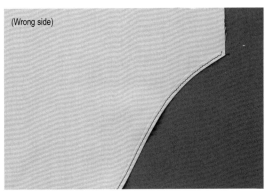

1   Fold the fabric edge 0.3–0.5 cm on the wrong side and staystitch. Use a standard zigzag presser foot and sew while folding the fabric edge with an awl.

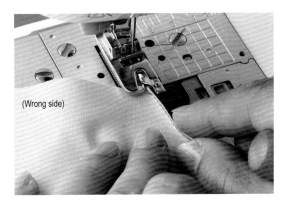

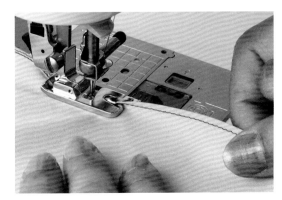

2   Switch to a rolled hem foot and wrap the one-fold fabric edge around the curled part of the foot.

3   Sew the edge by feeding it in a standing position into the foot.

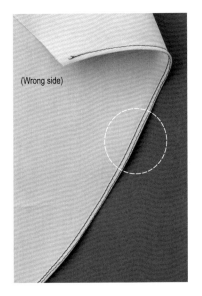

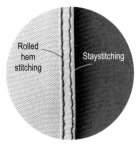

4   The completed hem. The wrong side has staystitching and rolled hem stitching while the right side only has the rolled hem stitching. You can remove the staystitching if you prefer.

Sewing a corner...fabric: cotton broadcloth

(Wrong side)

Paper

1   Make a rolled hem on one side, then double fold the top edge of the next side. The seam allowance at the upper end will overlap, so temporarily fasten it in place with fabric glue, then place paper (pattern paper or tracing paper) under the fabric and place both under the presser foot.

(Wrong side)

2   Follow steps **2–4** on p. 23 for **Sewing in a straight line**. Because the seam allowance at the starting edge is thick, the needle will have a hard time proceeding. Turn the flywheel of the sewing machine to sew one stitch at a time.

3   The completed hem.

Fabric glue

Handy for using as a temporary fastener instead of marking pins or basting.

Sewing in a circle...fabric: cotton broadcloth

Method of sewing rolled hems on circular pieces like sleeves and cuffs.

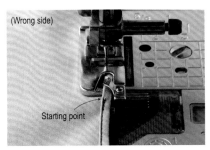

(Wrong side)

Starting point

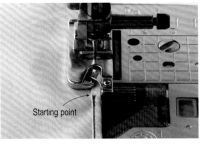

Starting point

Overlapped stitches

1   Following the same steps for **Sewing in a direct line** on p. 23, sew a rolled hem until you have almost returned to the starting point. Sew right up to the starting stitches, then stop with the needle down through the fabric.

2   Keep the needle down and raise the presser foot, removing the fabric edge that is wound around the curled part and place it under the foot. Lower the foot again and continue sewing to overlap the starting stitches.

3   The completed hem.

Side cutter foot

●Presser foot that does overcast stitches while cutting the end of the fabric. When the cutting width is small, it creates difficulties, so add 1 cm or more to the seam allowance when cutting the fabric.
●Not for thin fabrics like cotton lawn.

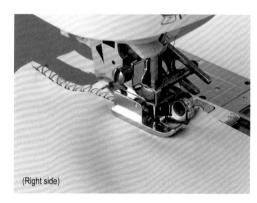

(Right side)

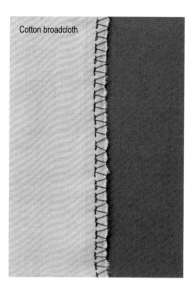

Cotton broadcloth

Gathering foot

●Presser foot for gathering and stitching at the same time. Suitable from fabric for thin to thick.
●The amount of gathering can change depending on the fabric, so do test sewing to confirm. You will also need to practice to get a good finish as it is difficult to create an equal amount of gathering.

Sewing method

Move the fabric (lace) to be gathered to the right side and place it under the presser foot. Place the main fabric (cotton broadcloth) that won't be gathered on the lace wrong side out. Insert the edges of the both pieces into the foot groove, and gather the lace as you sew.

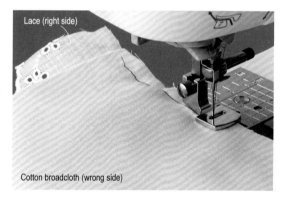

Lace (right side)

Cotton broadcloth (wrong side)

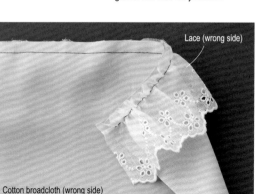

Lace (wrong side)

Cotton broadcloth (wrong side)

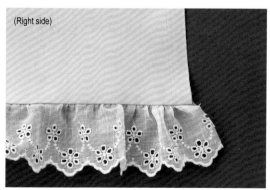

(Right side)

Buttonhole foot

●Presser foot for creating buttonholes. Set the button on the foot and the buttonhole is automatically created to match the size of the button.

Creating the buttonhole

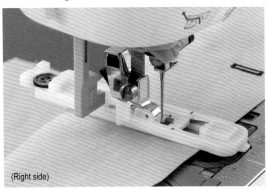

(Right side)

1 Mark the buttonhole position on the right side of the fabric (the diameter + thickness of the button), lower the needle on the starting position for stitching, and start sewing.

2 The automatically sewn buttonhole.

3 To prevent excessive cutting, fasten a marking pin on the edge of the buttonhole, and cut by inserting a seam ripper in the center of the seam.

4 The completed buttonhole.

Seam ripper

Ways to use an awl

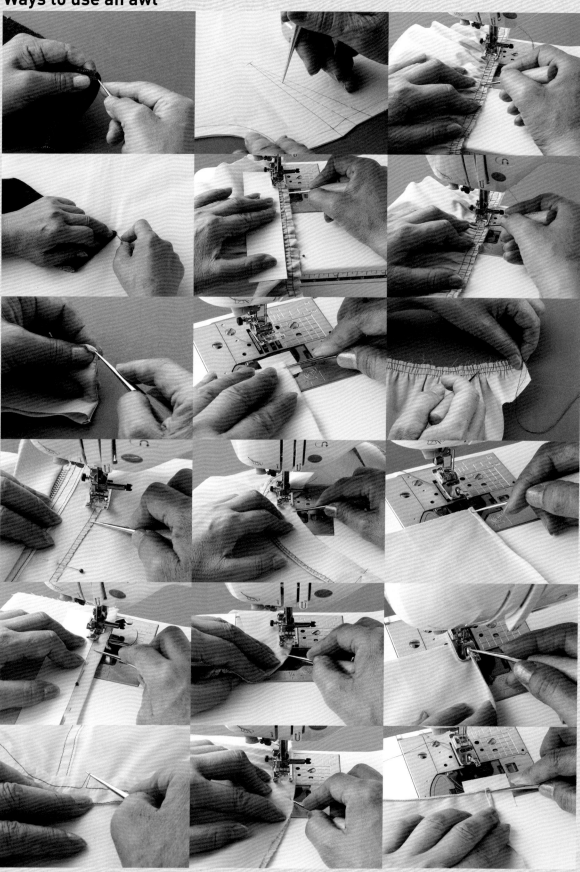

TAILORING
TECHNIQUES

Tailoring techniques

Neckline tailoring

- Round neck: facing (p. 32)
- Round neck: bias (p. 35)
- Round neck: facing and lining (p. 38)
- V-neck: bias (p. 40)

Collar tailoring

- V-neck: facing and lining (p. 43)
- Shirt collar (p. 45)
- Shirt collar with collar stand (p. 53)

Slit tailoring

- Slash placket: facing (p. 57)
- Slash placket: piping (p. 58)
- Partial button placket (p. 60)
- Simple hidden button placket (p. 62)
- Sleeve placket and cuff (p. 64)
- Concealed zipper opening (p. 67)
- Concealed zipper placket: panel cut lines (p. 71)
- Zipper opening: side of skirt (p. 72)
- Front zipper opening on pants (p. 75)

Pocket tailoring

●Front button placket on pants: lining (p. 79)

●Patch pocket: square (p. 81)

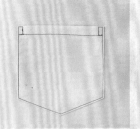

●Patch pocket: angled (p. 83)

●Patch pocket: curved (p. 84)

●Side seam pocket: French seam and side stitching (p. 85)

●French seam pocket: open side seam (p. 88)

●Piping pocket: one pocket bag (p. 90)

●Piping pocket: two pocket bags and button fastening (p. 94)

Sleeve tailoring

●Puff sleeve (p. 97)

●Armhole for shirt sleeve (p. 100)

●Armhole for shirt sleeve: flat-felled seam (p. 102)

●Armhole for shirt sleeve: French seam (p. 104)

●Armhole with set-in sleeve: shirring (p. 105)

Pleat tailoring

●Folding methods for pleats (p. 108)

Knit fabric tailoring

●Knit fabric round neck: common fabric tape (p. 112)

●Knit fabric round neck: adding neckline fabric (p. 114)

●Attaching rib-knit to the hem (p. 116)

Round neck: facing...fabric: cotton broadcloth

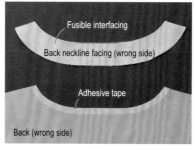

Fusible interfacing
Back neckline facing (wrong side)
Adhesive tape
Back (wrong side)

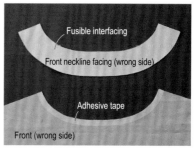

Fusible interfacing
Front neckline facing (wrong side)
Adhesive tape
Front (wrong side)

1   For the bodice and the facing, cut the neckline a seam allowance of 1 cm. On the front and back of the bodice neckline, apply adhesive tape to the wrong side, and attach fusible interfacing to the wrong side of both the front and back of the neckline facing.

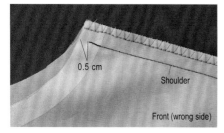

0.5 cm
Shoulder
Front (wrong side)

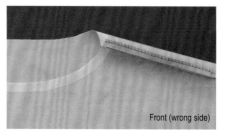

Front (wrong side)

2   Place the front and back bodice wrong side out and sew the shoulder. To prevent the seam allowance slipping, leave a 0.5 cm gap at the end of the stitching. Overcast stitch (or zigzag stitch) the seam allowance of the two fabric pieces together.

3   Fold the shoulder seam allowance of the bodice toward the back and neaten with an iron.

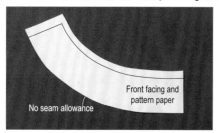

Front facing and pattern paper
No seam allowance

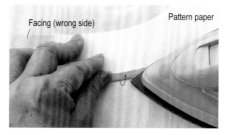

Facing (wrong side)
Pattern paper

4   Using paper about the thickness of a postcard, cut a pattern for the front and back facing that has the seam allowance cut off.

5   For both the front and back facing, place the step 4 pattern paper on the wrong side, and fold the seam allowance at the edge with the iron.

Applying fusible interfacing

- First apply fusible interfacing to some leftover fabric from the fabric being used to check the texture of interfacing after it has been applied.
- To ensure that the adhesive coming from the core does not come in contact with the iron, place a piece of pattern paper between the iron and the fabric. You can also use an iron cover to iron the interfacing.

Iron cover

Attach to bottom

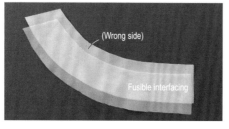

(Wrong side)
Fusible interfacing

1   Cut the fusible interfacing to the same size as the facing, and layer the adhesive side of the fusible interfacing (the rough side) on the wrong side of the facing.

2   Firmly press with the iron. Lift and move the iron without letting it slip, and press evenly over the entire piece.

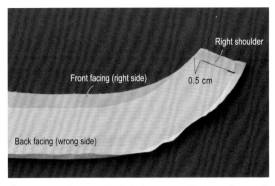

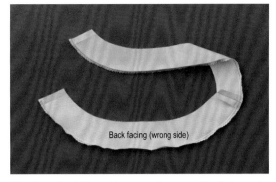

6   Place the front and back facing wrong side out and sew only the right shoulder. To prevent the seam allowance slipping, leave a 0.5 cm gap at the end of the stitching on the neckline. Stop sewing one stitch before the fold of the outer edge.

7   Open the right shoulder seam allowance of the facing and sew the outer seam allowance with overcast stitching.

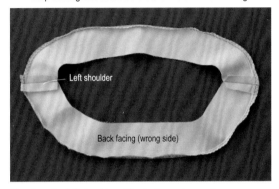

8   Sew the left shoulder of the facing and open the seam allowance.

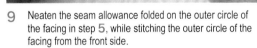

9   Neaten the seam allowance folded on the outer circle of the facing in step 5, while stitching the outer circle of the facing from the front side.

10   At the neckline of the bodice, layer the facing wrong side out so it matches up with the shoulders, front, and back, then fasten with a marking pin.

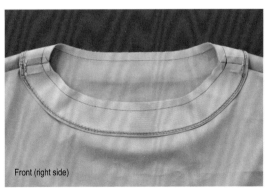

11   Sew the neckline in a circle. When beginning to sew from the shoulder, in places where it curves a lot, use the 1 cm scale (seam allowance width) to straighten the fabric while sewing.

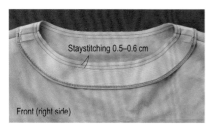

12 Roughly staystitch 0.5–0.6 cm from the seam on the seam allowance, using the width of the presser foot as a guide. This staystitching is a guideline so that you can cleanly cut the seam allowance.

13 Cut the seam allowance along the staystitching.

14 Fold and iron the neckline seam allowance from the seam toward the bodice.

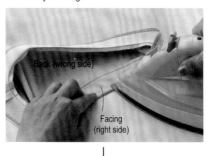

↓

15 Return the facing to the wrong side of the bodice, and while lightly holding the facing, iron the neckline. Use your left fingers to even out the fabric and just use the tip of the iron to flatten the neckline only.

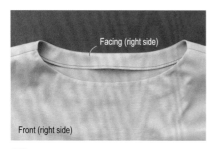

16 The completely ironed neckline.

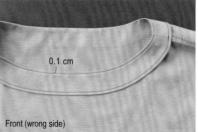

17 Leaving the bodice, turn back the neckline seam allowance toward the facing, and machine stitch only the facing and the seam allowance, from the right side of the facing.

18 Cross stitch or blindstitch the edge of the facing to the shoulder seam.

19 The completed neckline.

Round neck: bias ...fabric: cotton broadcloth

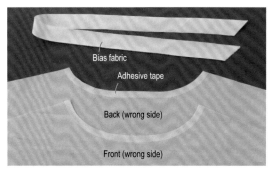

1   On the wrong side, apply adhesive tape of the neckline seam allowance of the front and back bodice. Cut the bias fabric for the neckline to 2.5–3 cm in width and add 5–10 cm in length to the neckline measurement.

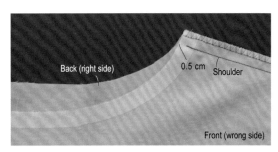

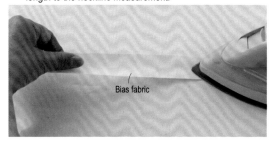

2   Place the shoulders of the front and back bodice wrong side out and sew. To prevent the seam allowance on the neckline slipping, leave a 0.5 cm gap in the stitching at the end of the fabric. Overcast stitch (or zigzag stitch) the seam allowances of both pieces together, then fold over to the back.

3   Lightly stretch the bias fabric with an iron.

Applying adhesive tape

● Adhesive tape is applied to necklines, armholes, and pockets to prevent stretching. It can be used instead of fusible interfacing, adding strength to places to be cut.
● The adhesive tape is attached to the stitch line and adhered to the seam allowance. As an example, while 1.2 cm adhesive tape is used on a 1 cm seam allowance, when using 1 cm tape, shift it inward from the fabric edge by 0.2 cm to attach it to the stitch line.

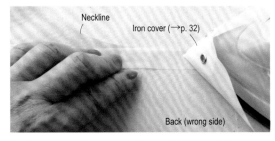

1   Evenly place the tape onto the straight line of stitching.

2   Along curves, press the bottom of the tape flat to the neckline with the tip of the iron. The top edge of the tape will pucker. Don't pull to flatten it; let it bunch a little.

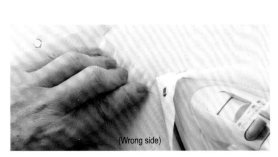

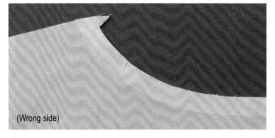

3   Make the puckered sections uniform by rubbing down with your finger and pressing them with the iron.

4   The neckline pressed and finished.

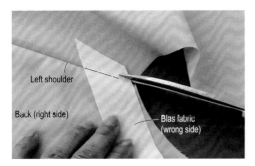

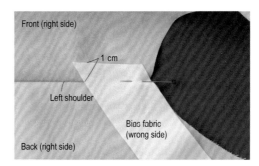

4   Place the bias fabric wrong side out on the back of the bodice starting at the left shoulder. Slide the neckline edge 2 cm from the left shoulder and cut the bias fabric using the shoulder seam as a guideline.

5   Make the cut edges from step 4 parallel with the left shoulder seam and shift 1 cm forward, then fasten the bias fabric to the shoulder with a marking pin.

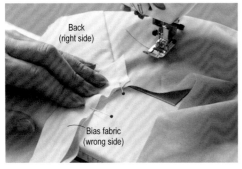

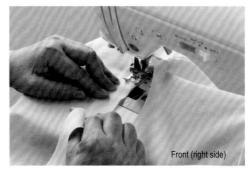

6   Place the bias fabric about 4 cm from the shoulder at the position of the finished edge of the bodice neckline, then fasten with a marking pin. This is the place where you will start sewing.

7   Start by doing two to three reverse stitches from the position of the marking pin. As you join the bias fabric to the neckline edge, sew the bias fabric so it is straight with the neckline (the machine stitching).

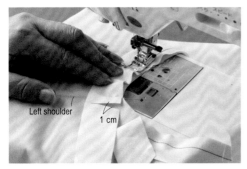

8   Sew in a circle, then do two to three reverse stitches 4–5 cm before reaching the left shoulder. From there to the shoulder, follow step 6 to apply the bias fabric to the neckline, then fasten with a marking pin on the shoulder. After that, make the bias fabric parallel to the shoulder seam, adding a 1 cm seam allowance, then cut the excess.

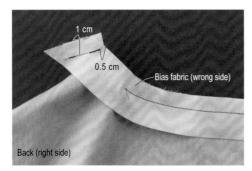

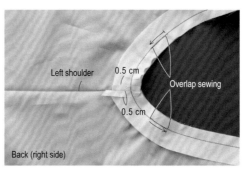

9   Turn the left shoulder of the bias fabric wrong side out, and sew giving a 1 cm seam allowance.

10   Cut and open the seam allowance in step 9 to 0.5 cm and sew the remainder of the neckline. Sew the beginning and the end overlapping the stitching in step 8 by about 2 cm.

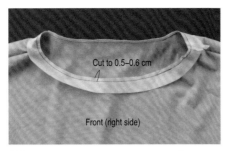

11 Staystitch at the 0.5–0.6 cm seam allowance side of the neckline stitching, then cut the seam allowance along that stitching (→p. 34 steps 12, 13).

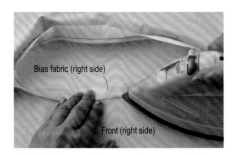

12 Fold the neckline seam allowance onto the bias fabric side and iron from the front.

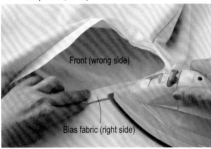

13 Fold the bias fabric on the wrong side of the bodice, and holding the bias fabric, smooth it out with an iron.

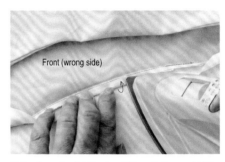

14 Open the fold in step 13, and align and fold the bias fabric edge along the stitch line so that it wraps around the neckline seam allowance.

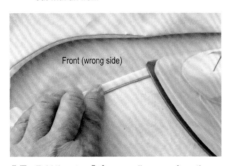

15 Fold the step 14 seam allowance from the step 13 standing fold toward the bodice, ironing it once more to neaten it.

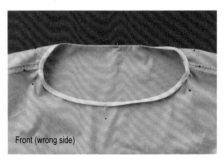

16 Fasten the double fold bias fabric with a marking pin.

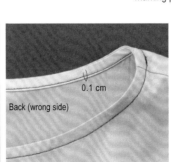

17 Stitch the bias fabric edge. Start sewing from the left shoulder.

18 The completed neckline.

Round neck: facing and lining...fabric: thick wool

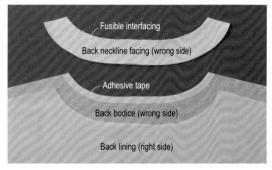

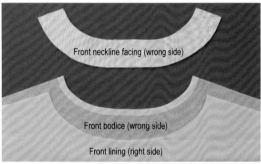

1 Apply adhesive tape to the wrong side neckline both on the front and back, and apply fusible interfacing to the inside of the facing.

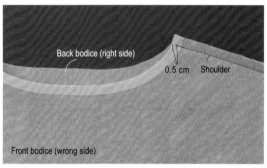

2 Align the front and back shoulder wrong side out and sew. To prevent the neckline seam allowance slipping, leave a 0.5 cm gap at the end of the stitching. Open the seam allowance.

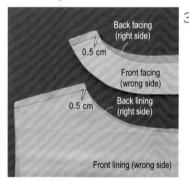

3 Turn the front and back parts of the facing, bodice, and lining wrong side out and sew the shoulders. Leave a 0.5 cm gap at the end of stitching on each neckline part. Open the shoulder seam allowance of the facing, and fold the lining seam allowance to the back.

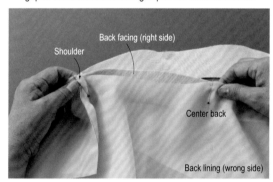

4 Place the lining fabric wrong side out on the outer edge of the facing, fastening with a marking pin on the right and left shoulders, as well as the center front and back.

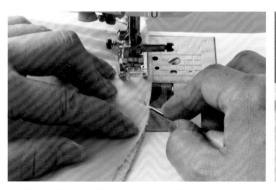

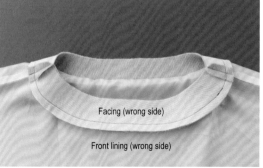

5 Sew the lining and the facing together. The lining can catch easily when placed down for sewing, so begin sewing from the left shoulder with the lining on top. Join the two fabric edges, pressing with an awl as you sew, keeping the stitching straight.

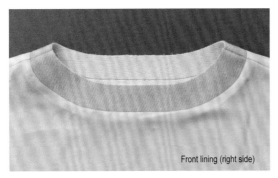

6 Turn the step 5 seam allowance toward the lining and smooth with iron.

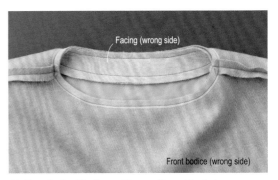

7 Turn the front bodice and the neckline of the facing wrong side out to sew.

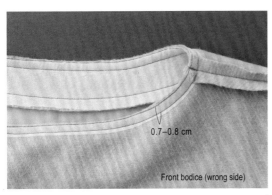

8 Roughly staystitch at 0.7–0.8 cm from the seam allowance of the neckline seam.

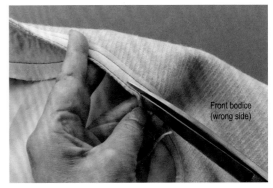

9 Cut the seam allowance away from the staystitching. Do this while looking at it from the right side of the bodice.

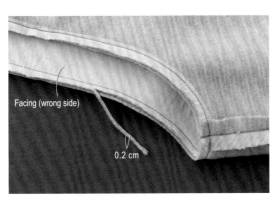

10 Cut a further 0.2 cm, on only the seam allowance of the facing, to create a gap between the seam allowance of the front bodice and the facing.

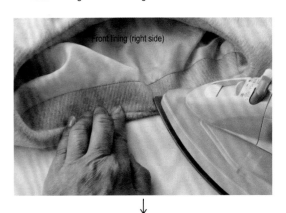

11 Return to the right side out and iron the neckline. When ironing, press the facing down hard with your fingers and pull it back, then release slightly to about 0.2 cm, then iron.

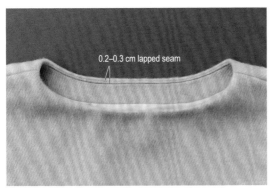

12 Machine stitch only the facing and seam allowance (→p. 34 step 17) and smooth out with an iron. The completed neckline.

V-neck: bias...fabric: cotton broadcloth

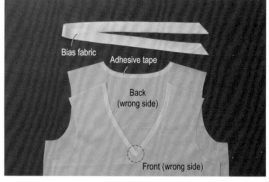

1 Place adhesive tape along the wrong side of the front and back part neckline seam allowance marking the V end point. Cut the bias fabric 2.5–3 cm in width, and add 5–10 cm to the neckline length.

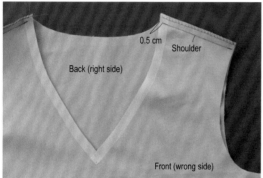

2 Place the shoulder of the front and back bodice wrong side out and sew. To prevent the neckline seam allowance slipping, leave a 0.5 cm gap at the end of stitching. Overcast stitch (or zigzag stitch) the seam allowances and fold toward the back.

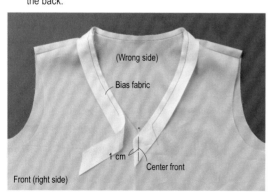

→

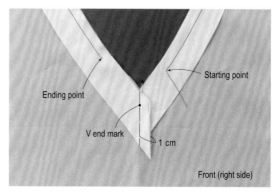

3 Lightly stretch the bias fabric with the iron (→p. 35 step 3). Place the bias fabric wrong side out onto the neckline of the bodice, and sew up to 4–5 cm from the V ending mark. At this time, add 1 cm to the seam allowance overlapping the V point, cut the excess, and copy the V ending mark to the bias fabric.

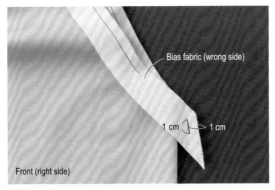

Bias fabric (wrong side)

1 cm ◁ 1 cm

Front (right side)

4 Turn both ends of the bias fabric wrong side out, and sew 1 cm from the mark toward the bottom (adding 0.2–0.3 cm to the finished width of the bias fabric).

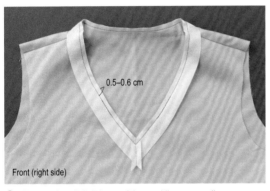

0.5–0.6 cm

Front (right side)

6 Staystitch to 0.5–0.6 cm of the neckline seam allowance, then cut the seam allowance from the seam (→p. 34 steps 12, 13).

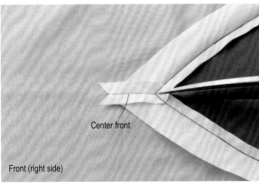

Center front

Front (right side)

8 Open the step 7 fold, and leaving the bias fabric, cut the seam allowance on the bodice V part.

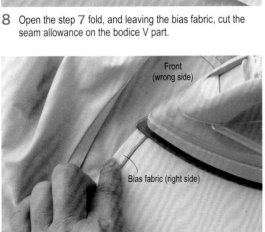

Front (wrong side)

Bias fabric (right side)

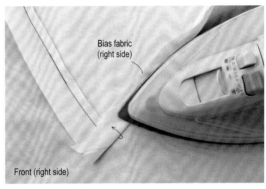

1 cm ◁ 1 cm
Stitch finely

Front (right side)

5 Open the step 4 seam allowances, and sew the remaining V part of the neckline. Finely stitch the 1 cm to the left and right of the V end mark.

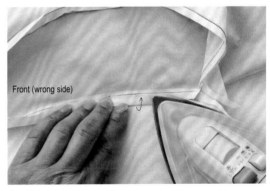

Bias fabric (right side)

Front (right side)

7 Turn only the bias fabric back to the right side and fold from the seam with an iron.

Front (wrong side)

9 Line up the edges of the bias fabric onto the neckline seam and fold them to wrap over the seam allowance.

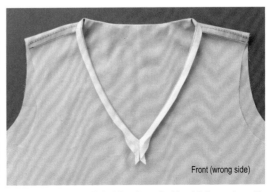

Front (wrong side)

10 Turn the wrapped seam allowance to the wrong side of the bodice, and while slightly holding down the bias fabric, neaten with an iron, leaving out the V part.

11 Finish the V neckline. First, double-fold one side of the bias fabric V part.

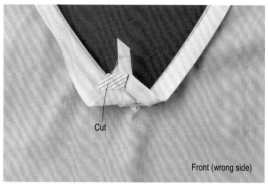

12 Cut the end of the step 11 folded bias fabric on the wrong side as shown in the picture.

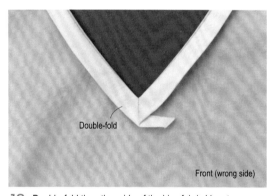

13 Double-fold the other side of the bias fabric V part.

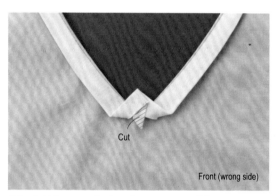

14 Fold the protruding bias fabric from step 13 onto the back as shown in the picture and trim the excess.

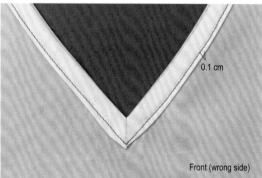

15 Smooth with the iron and stitch the bias fabric edge. The completed neckline.

V-neck: facing and lining...wool georgette

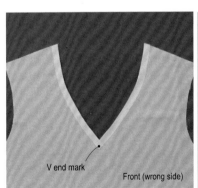

V end mark
Front (wrong side)

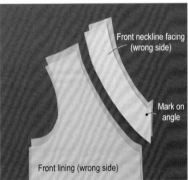

Front neckline facing
(wrong side)

Mark on
angle

Front lining (wrong side)

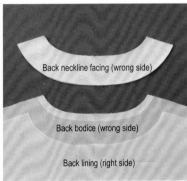

Back neckline facing (wrong side)

Back bodice (wrong side)

Back lining (right side)

1 Apply adhesive tape to the wrong sides of the front and back bodice part neckline seam allowances, and add fusible interfacing to the wrong sides of the facing, making an end mark on each V. For the lining, even when the center of the front bodice is cut on the fold, sewing is easier when the facing and lining have seams.

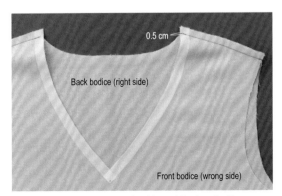

0.5 cm

Back bodice (right side)

Front bodice (wrong side)

2 Align the front and back shoulders of the front bodice wrong side out and sew. To prevent the neckline seam allowance slipping, leave a 0.5 cm gap at the end of stitching. Open the seam allowance.

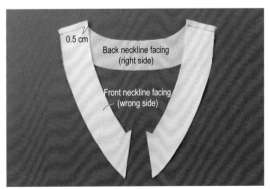

0.5 cm

Back neckline facing
(right side)

Front neckline facing
(wrong side)

3 Turn the shoulders of the front and back neckline facing wrong side out and sew, leaving a 0.5 cm gap at the end of stitching at the top of the neckline. Open the seam allowance.

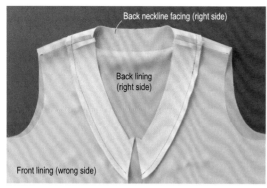

Back neckline facing (right side)

Back lining
(right side)

Front lining (wrong side)

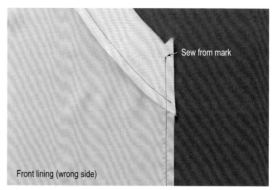

Sew from mark

Front lining (wrong side)

4   Sew the lining shoulder and fold the seam allowance to the back. Next, sew the facing and the lining together (→p. 38 steps 4, 5).

5   Continue sewing the center front of the facing and lining. Sew from the V end mark down the neckline, then open the allowance.

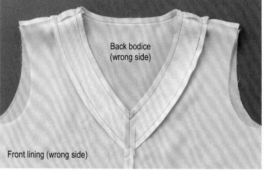

Back bodice
(wrong side)

Front lining (wrong side)

6   With the bodice and facing wrong sides out, sew the neckline. Begin sewing from the V end mark, going around once in a circle and overlapping the starting stitches at the end by 2 cm.

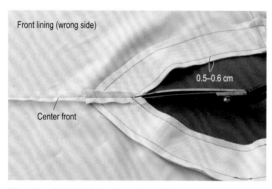

Front lining (wrong side)

0.5–0.6 cm

Center front

7   Staystitch 0.5–0.6 cm into the neckline seam allowance, trim the allowance from the seam (→p. 34 steps 12,13). Leaving the facing seam allowance, make cuts into the seam allowance of bodice V part.

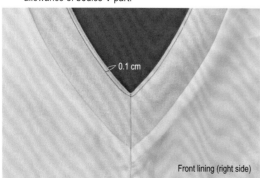

0.1 cm

Front lining (right side)

8   Turn right side out, iron the collar avoiding the facing, apply lapped seam to facing and seam allowance (→p. 34 steps 14–17). Completed.

Collar tailoring
Shirt collar...fabric: thin denim

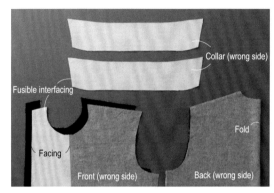

1 Cut the collar with a 1 cm seam allowance and apply fusible interfacing on the wrong sides of the collar and the front-end facing.

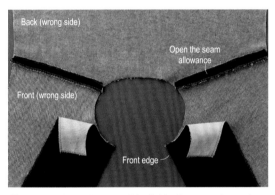

2 Fold the front edge toward the finished seam and smooth with an iron, then sew the shoulders together and open the seam allowance.

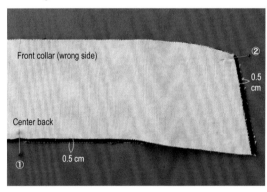

3 Layer the two fabric pieces for the collar, shifting the top fabric edge back 0.5 cm and fastening with marking pins at the center back (①) and center front (②). The top part pinned at 0.5 cm will be the front collar. When using cotton broad-type fabric, shift the edge back by 0.2–0.3 cm.

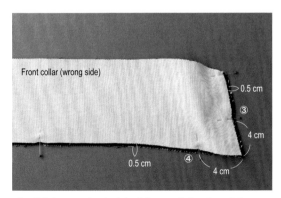

4 Shift the top edge back by 0.5 cm and align them flat, fastening them with a marking pin at approximately 4 cm from the points (③, ④) of the collar.

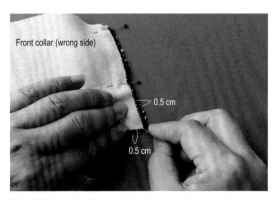

5 Shift the collar tip parallel to 0.5 cm and fasten with a marking pin at the collar tip.

Front collar (wrong side)

② ③ ① ④ ⑤

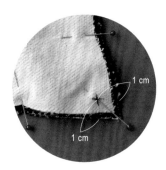
1 cm
1 cm

6   Insert marking pins in the same way in the remaining half, and mark the end points of the collar tips. When the collar is folded back, this shifted part will add slack to the front collar.

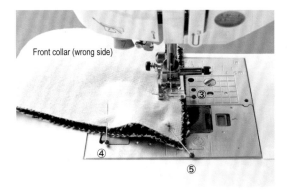
Front collar (wrong side)
③ ④ ⑤

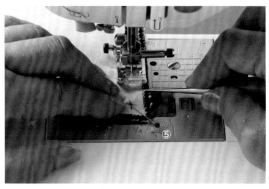
⑤

7   Place the front collar and sew the outer rim at a seam allowance of 1 cm from the edge of the back collar (the piece underneath). First, sew flat the two pieces between marking pins ②–③.

8   Between pins ③–⑤, make the slack in the front collar uniform and press down the fabric with your left hand. Then use an awl when sewing to press down the edge.

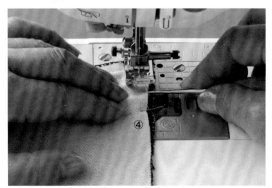
④

9   Change the direction of sewing at the edge of pin ⑤, and sew up to pin ④ in the same way as for step 8 above.

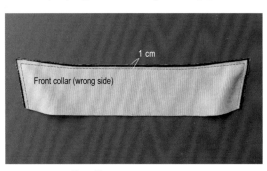
1 cm
Front collar (wrong side)

Back collar (wrong side)

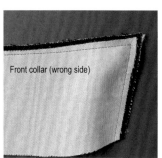
Front collar (wrong side)

10   For pins ④ to ① sew the two pieces flat, then sew the other two the same way. Sew up the collar sides, leaving the slack.

11　The seam allowance of the collar tip is cut at an angle.

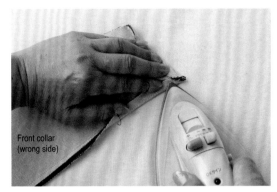

12　Fold the seam of the outer seam allowance on the collar toward the front collar. In particular, make sure to fold the collar tip and firmly press with an iron.

→

13　Turn the collar right side out. Press the seam allowance folded at the collar tip firmly with your fingers, to turn it right side out.

14　Make sure to pull out the very tip of the collar with an awl, then smooth into shape.

15　Slightly hold down the back collar and smooth it with an iron.

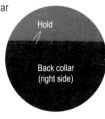

16　Hold the collar as shown in the picture, and check the left and right shape of the collar points.

17 Stitch from the outer rim of the front collar side.

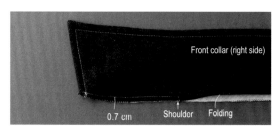

18 Align the edges of the front and back collars and staystitch along the seam allowance up to the shoulder mark. For the part connected to the back of the shirt, fold only the seam allowance of the front collar inward with an iron.

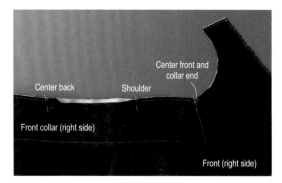

19 Avoiding the front edge facing, align the wrong sides of the back collar and the back of the bodice, then fasten with marking pins at the center front and back and the shoulder.

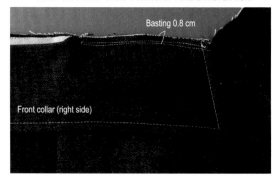

20 From the collar end to the shoulder, baste along the seam allowance of the collar line.

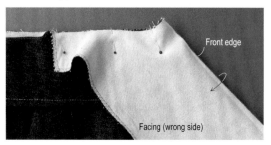

21 Fold the front edge facing wrong side out, layer it on the collar and fasten with a marking pin.

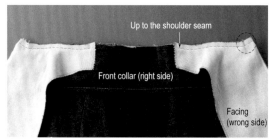
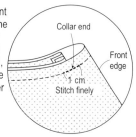

22 Attach the collar to the front neckline by sewing from the front edge to the shoulder seam. Stitch finely around 0.5 cm from the collar end, and stop sewing where the shoulder joins the shoulder seam.

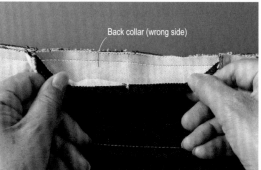

23 Sew the back neckline from the shoulder. Leave the front collar at this time, and only sew the back collar and the neckline of the bodice from shoulder to shoulder.

24   Turn the facing right side out, then match up the left and right collars to check the collar width. If the widths are different, sew to adjust.

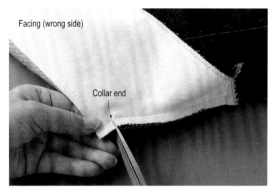

Facing (wrong side)

Collar end

25   Return the facing wrong side out, and cut into the seam allowance of the collar edge on the bodice.

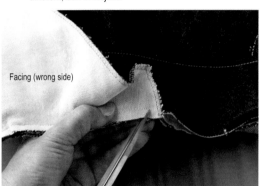

Facing (wrong side)

26   Make angled cuts into the seam allowances where sewing stopped at the shoulder of step 22. The fabric pieces are layered, so if cutting is difficult cut two to three pieces at a time in order, starting from the top.

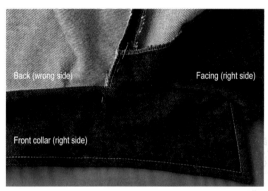

Back (wrong side)
Facing (right side)
Front collar (right side)

27   Return the facing right side out and smooth it, then lay the front facing shoulder to the shoulder of the bodice and fasten in place with a marking pin.

Stitch

Back (wrong side)

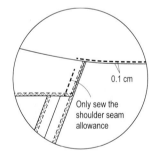

0.1 cm

Only sew the shoulder seam allowance

28   Fold the back seam allowance of the front collar and fasten it with a stitch. Stitch the shoulder seam allowance of the front facing just behind the shoulder seam allowance to avoid the bodice and sew the neckline as far as possible.

29   The completed collar.

Reverse stitching a small circular collar with collar tips...fabric: cotton broadcloth

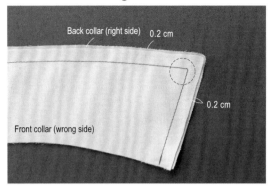

Back collar (right side) 0.2 cm

0.2 cm

Front collar (wrong side)

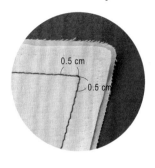

0.5 cm

0.5 cm

1   Turn the two pieces of fabric wrong side out, shifting the top edge back 0.2 cm, then sew (→pp. 45, 46 steps 3–10). Stitch finely 0.5 cm in the front and back of the collar tip at this time. The small circle part in the picture shows where you will cut the seam allowance when machine stitching, so to prevent the seam fraying and also make sewing the curve easier, sew fine stitches here.

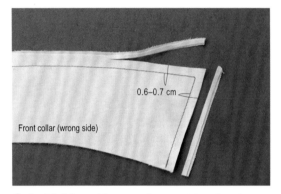

0.6–0.7 cm

Front collar (wrong side)

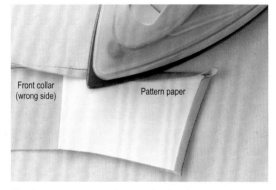

Front collar
(wrong side)   Pattern paper

2   Cut 0.6–0.7 cm of the seam allowance at the collar edge.

3   Create pattern paper for the collar tip using paper the thickness of a postcard. Overlay that pattern paper on the wrong side of front collar, then fold over the seam allowance of the edge with the iron, leaving the collar tip up. Use the pattern paper to evenly smooth out the collar tip shape.

Pattern
paper

4   While applying the pattern paper, open the seam allowance folded at the collar tip, then cut the tip, leaving a small circular seam allowance around 0.1 cm from the stitching.

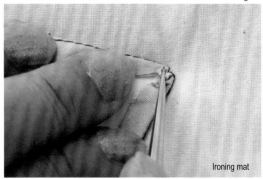

Ironing mat

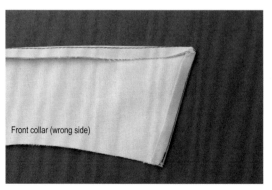

Front collar (wrong side)

5   Fold the small circular seam allowance with an awl from the seam, and firmly press it with an iron.

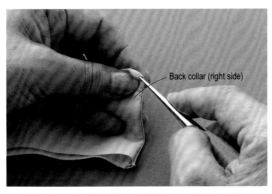

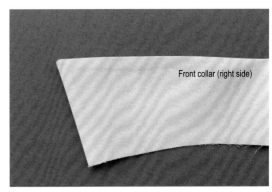

6   Turn the collar right side out. Pull the small circle of the collar tip out with an awl and smooth it into shape.

7   While slightly holding the back collar, neaten the outer edge with the iron.

Sewing sharp collar tips... fabric: chiffon georgette

When you make pointed collar tips with a smooth, thin fabric like chiffon georgette, the collar points become very thin. To make the collar look thicker, extend the collar tip a little over the finishing line, as shown in picture A, for a smarter finish. Additionally, seams can easily pucker on chiffon georgette, so apply paper (such as kraft paper or tracing paper) while sewing.

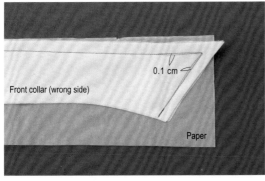

A   Chiffon georgette collar where the seam allowance of collar point is extended around 0.1 cm over the finishing line.

→

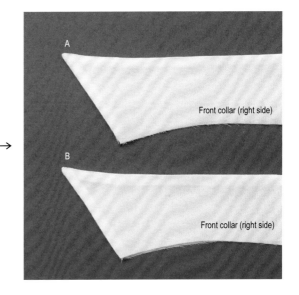

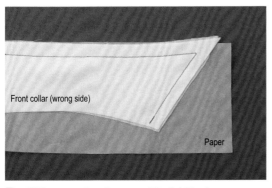

B   Chiffon georgette collar sewn at the finishing line.

Sewing a round collar...fabric: silk taffeta

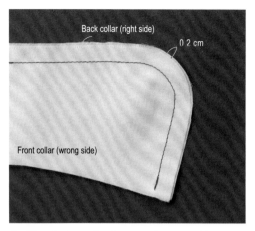

1 Place the two collar pieces together wrong side out, then shift the top edge back 0.2 cm, and sew (→pp. 45, 46 steps 3–10).

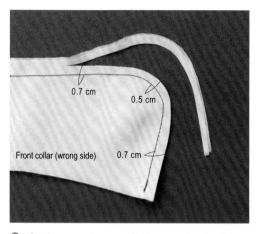

2 Cut the seam allowance. Cut the curved part to 0.5 cm and the straight part to 0.7 cm.

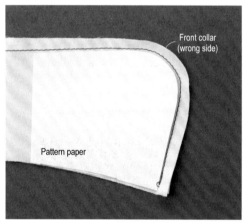

3 Make pattern paper for the curved part using paper the thickness of a postcard, and overlay it on the inside of the front collar.

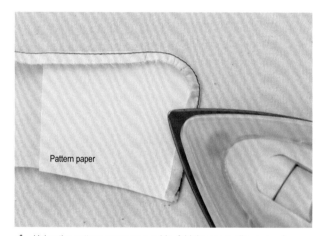

4 Using the pattern paper as a guide, fold the seam allowance of the collar edge from the seam. For the curved part, to prevent unbalanced lines on the seam allowance, make the creases uniform, then iron while neatly shaping the curve.

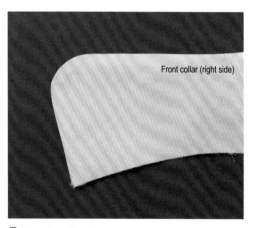

5 Turn the collar right side out and smooth with an iron while slightly pushing down the back collar.

Collar tailoring
Shirt collar with collar stand… fabric: cotton broadcloth

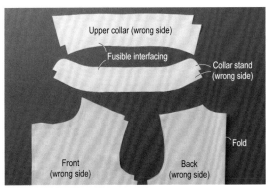

1 Attach fusible interfacing on the wrong side of the collar stand and upper collar.

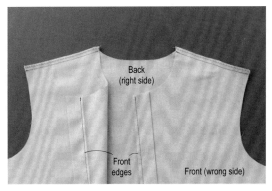

2 For the bodice, smooth it out by double-folding the front and sewing the shoulders together. For the seam allowance, overcast stitch (or zigzag stitch) the two pieces and fold toward the back.

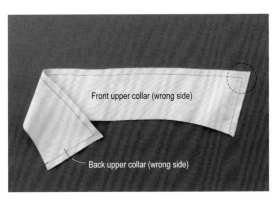

3 Shift the top outer edge of the front upper collar by at 0.2 cm and sew them together (→pp. 45, 46 steps 3–10).

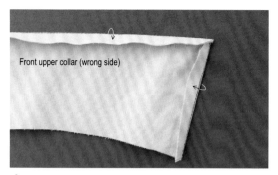

4 Cut the seam allowance of the upper collar at an angle (→p. 47 step 11), then fold the edge of seam allowance from the seam toward the front collar side.

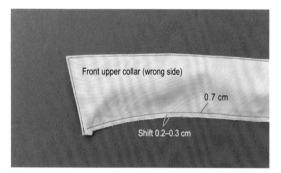

6 Shift the fabric edge of the front upper collar back 0.2–0.3 cm and machine stitch the bottom of the upper collar.

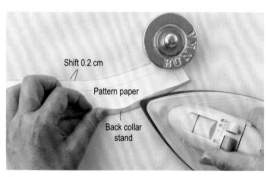

8 Lay the step 7 pattern paper on top of the other collar stand's wrong side, shift the upper end back 0.2 cm and fold the seam allowance of the bottom part with an iron. The folded seam allowance will be 0.2 cm smaller due to step 7. This will be the back collar stand.

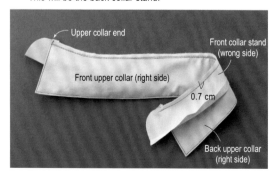

9 Align the front collar stand and back upper collar wrong sides out, and baste along the seam allowance.

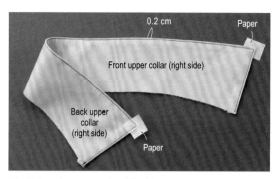

5 Return the upper collar right side out, then while lightly holding the back upper collar, smooth them out with the iron. The angle of the collar tips can make it difficult to sew. Attach paper (kraft paper or tracing paper) at the bottom to make sewing smoother then tear off the paper at the end.

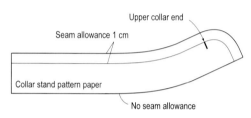

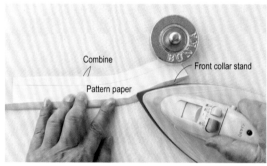

7 Create pattern paper for the collar stand using paper the thickness of a postcard. Overlay that pattern paper onto the wrong side of the collar stand, align the upper ends of the fabric and pattern paper, then fold the seam allowance of the lower part (part connected to the bodice) with an iron. This will be the front collar stand.

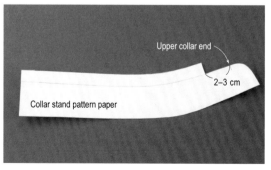

10 Cut the curved part of the seam allowance of the collar tip of the step 7 pattern paper.

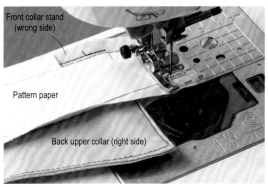

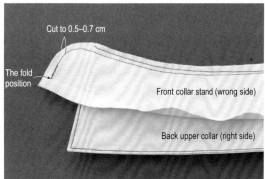

11 Match the wrong sides of the front upper collar of step 9 and the back collar stand, sandwiching the upper collar at the collar stand and sewing from the side of the front collar stand. In order to align the curved part of the left and right collar stand tips, apply the pattern paper from step 10 and sew, or apply the pattern paper before sewing, drawing the finishing line of the curved part and then sewing. Additionally, start and finish sewing at the fold position underneath the front collar stand. When sewing is complete, cut the seam allowance of the curve to 0.5–0.7 cm.

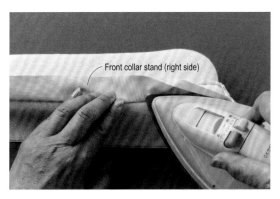

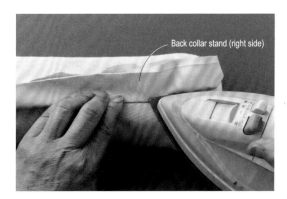

12 Return the front collar stand right side out and bring the seam allowance toward the collar stand part, smoothing out the area up to the upper collar end with the iron. To make sure that the iron does not touch the upper collar, use the end of the ironing board or a pressing ham.

13 Return the back collar stand right side out too, and iron as shown in step 12.

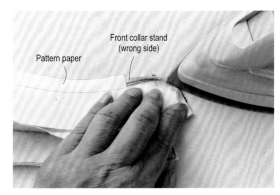

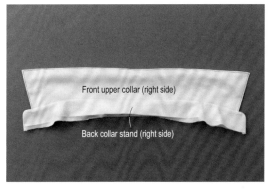

14 Lay the step 10 pattern paper on the wrong side of the front collar stand, then fold the seam allowance of the curve from the seam with the iron. Use the tip of the iron to uniformly balance the lines in the seam allowance.

15 Return the collar stand right side out and smooth it completely with the iron.

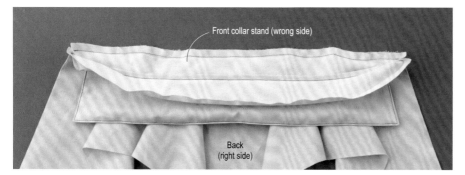

Front collar stand (wrong side)

Back
(right side)

16   Align the front collar stands and the neckline of the bodice wrong sides out, and the back collar stand, sew the collar. If you shift back the front edge of the collar stands 0.1–0.2 cm when joining the pieces the collar stands will not jut out when turned right side out.

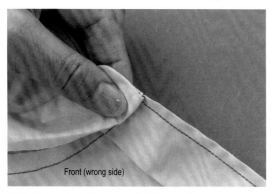

Front (wrong side)

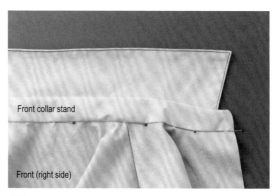

Front collar stand

Front (right side)

17   Return right side out and fold the step 16 seam allowance toward the collar stand, then neatly fold the seam allowance at the front edge of the collar stands.

18   Fold the seam allowance from the side with the back collar stand, then at the step 8 fold line, fasten with a marking pin onto the seam from the front collar stand part.

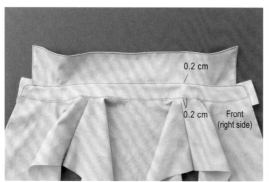

0.2 cm

0.2 cm   Front (right side)

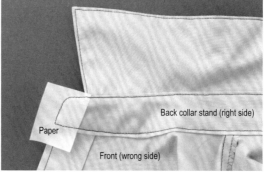

Back collar stand (right side)

Paper

Front (wrong side)

19   Stitch the area around the collar stand from the front side. Attach paper (such as kraft paper or tracing paper) to the back collar stand for sewing. You can feed the fabric more smoothly doing this and it prevents the curved part being stretched.

20   Tear the paper away from the collar stand tip, smooth the collar stand out with the iron and the collar is completed.

Slash placket: facing... fabric: wool georgette

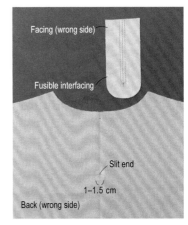

1 Attach fusible interfacing on the slit end of the wrong side of the back bodice, adding a mark to the slit end. For the facing, apply fusible interfacing to the wrong side and draw the finishing line of the placket.

2 Overcast stitch (or zigzag stitch) the outer edging of the facing, match the wrong sides of the facing and the back bodice, and sew the placket into a U shape. Make a fine stitch 0.5 cm from both sides of the slit end (→See figure).

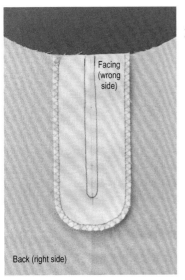

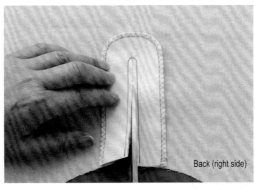

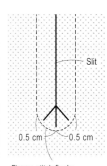

Figure: stitch finely

3 Cut the center where the U shape is sewn. The slit end is cut into an arrow shape.

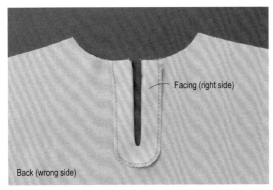

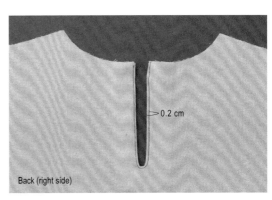

4 Return the facing toward the back bodice, lightly hold down the facing and then smooth it with the iron.

5 Stitch round the placket from the right side of the back bodice. The completed placket.

Slash placket: piping...fabric: chiffon georgette

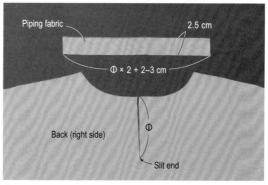

1 Cut to the slit end of the back bodice. For the piping fabric, when using fabric that is thin and soft, like chiffon georgette, it is easier to sew when cutting is done straight. When using fabric with tension, be it regular fabric or thinner, cut on the bias to make it easier to work with. Additionally, make the piping fabric 2–3 cm longer than the specified size, so it is easier to sew.

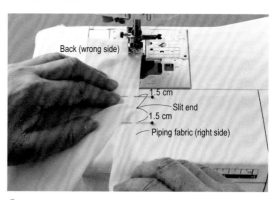

2 Straighten the back fabric after the cut is opened and place it wrong side out on the piping fabric, then fasten marking pins 1.5 cm at the top and bottom of the slit end.

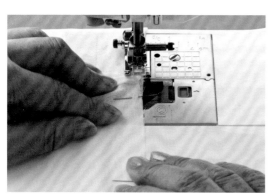

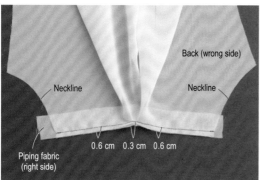

3 The width from the top edge to the marking pins is 0.6 cm. Stitch finely at a width of 0.3 cm between the pins.

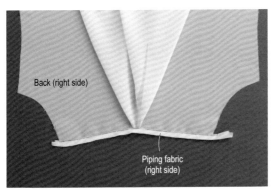

Back (right side)

Piping fabric
(right side)

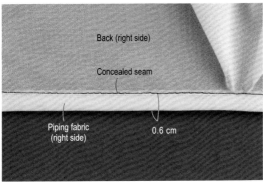

Back (right side)

Concealed seam

Piping fabric
(right side)

0.6 cm

4 Wrap the piping fabric around the seam allowance. Fold piping fabric with an iron at 0.6 cm for the right side and at 0.7 cm for the wrong side, then sew at the edge of folded piping from the right side. After smoothing it out with an iron, cut off the excess piping fabric.

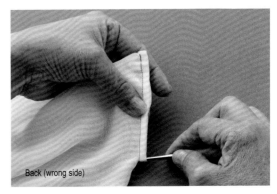

Back (wrong side)

5 Turn the placket piping wrong side out, insert an awl in the slit end, and pull down to smooth it out. This makes it easier to sew.

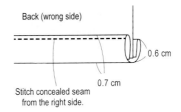

Back (wrong side)

0.6 cm

0.7 cm

Stitch concealed seam from the right side.

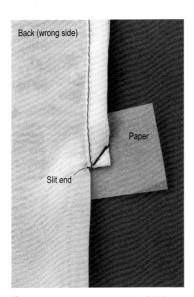

Back (wrong side)

Paper

Slit end

Back (right side)

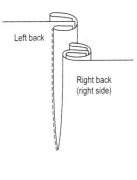

Left back

Right back
(right side)

6 Sew diagonally on the piping fabric at the slit end. Attach paper to the bottom (such as kraft paper or tracing paper), and stitch that three or four times.

7 Tear the paper away from the slit end and return right side out. Fold the right back piping to the wrong side of the bodice and smooth it out by ironing. The completed placket.

Partial button placket...fabric: cotton broadcloth

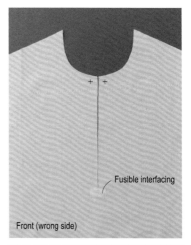

Fusible interfacing

Front (wrong side)

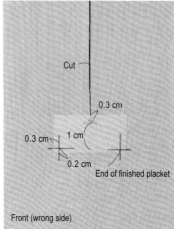

Cut

0.3 cm

0.3 cm   1 cm

0.2 cm

End of finished placket

Front (wrong side)

1 Apply fusible interfacing to the front
   bodice at the end of the line of the
   placket and cut in the middle up to
   1 cm above the end of the line.

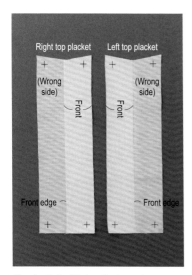

Right top placket   Left top placket

+   +   +   +

(Wrong   (Wrong
side)   side)

Front   Front

Front edge   Front edge

+   +   +   +

2 Apply fusible interfacing to the wrong
   side of the front of the top left and
   right placket.

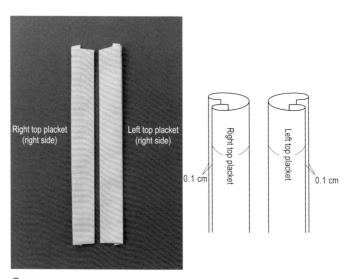

Right top placket   Left top placket
(right side)   (right side)

Right top placket   Left top placket

0.1 cm   0.1 cm

3 The seam allowance of the placket fabric is folded onto the wrong side
   with an iron at the bottom edge. This is done on both sides, and it is
   further folded in half right side out. When folding it in half, slide the front
   side of the placket back about 0.1 cm and fold.

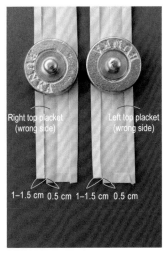

4 Cut the right top placket at the bottom of the back and the left top placket at the bottom of the back, as shown in the picture.

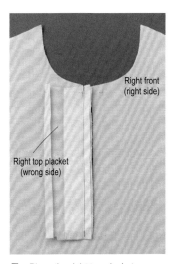

5 Place the right top placket on the right side of the right front bodice, with the wrong sides out, and sew.

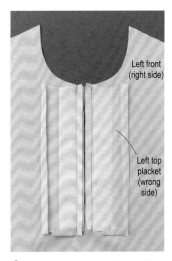

6 Place the left top placket on the right side of the left front bodice, with the wrong side out, and sew.

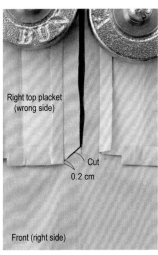

7 Make an angled cut at the end of the right top placket attached to the bodice, making sure to avoid the placket's seam allowance.

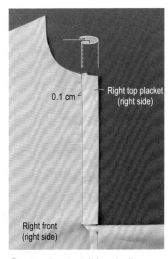

8 Avoiding the left front bodice, fold the right top placket over the seam allowance, and stitch on the edge of the placket.

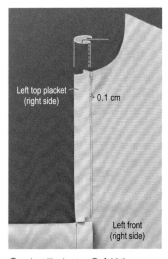

9 Just like in step 8, fold the left top placket over the seam allowance, and stitch the edge.

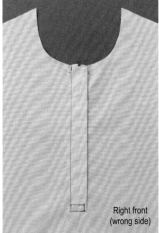

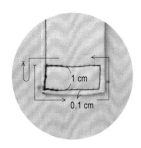

10 Move the right front up and overlay the left and right plackets, sew the bottom ends together. The completed placket.

Simple hidden button placket...fabric: cotton broadcloth

Pattern

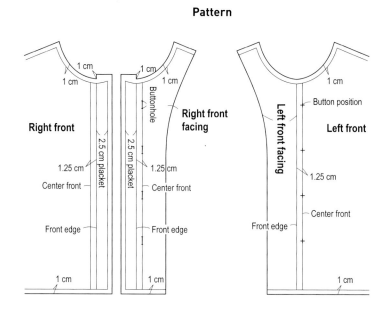

Right front

1 cm
1 cm
2.5 cm placket
1.25 cm
Center front
Front edge
1 cm

Buttonhole
1 cm
1 cm
2.5 cm placket
Right front facing
1.25 cm
Center front
Front edge
1 cm

Left front facing
1 cm
Button position
Left front
1.25 cm
Center front
Front edge
1 cm

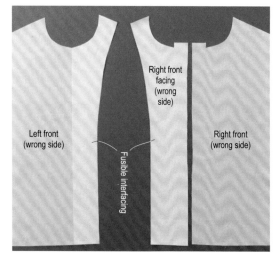

Left front (wrong side)

Right front facing (wrong side)

Right front (wrong side)

Fusible interfacing

1 Attach fusible interfacing on the wrong side of the right front facing and the wrong side of the facing part of the left front bodice.

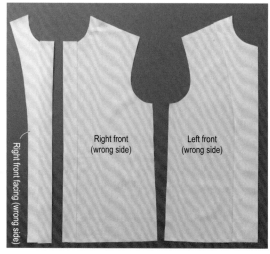

Right front facing (wrong side)

Right front (wrong side)

Left front (wrong side)

2 For the right front bodice and right front facing, the placket is folded on the wrong side with an iron, and the same for the facing part of the left front bodice.

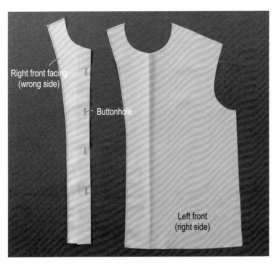

3   Overcast stitch (or zigzag stitch) the inside of both the left and right facing. For the right front facing, create a buttonhole while the placket is folded.

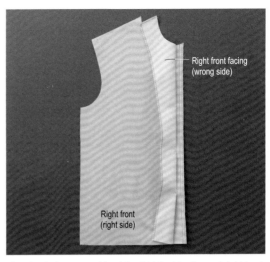

4   Match the wrong side of the right front bodice and right front facing, and sew the placket edges. Overcast stitch on both pieces of fabric for the seam allowance.

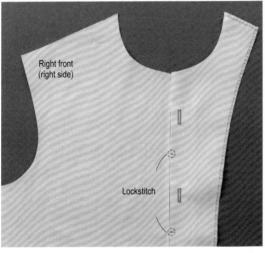

5   Lockstitch in the center of the buttonhole while avoiding the right front bodice. Make three to four horizontal stitches three to four times in the same place.

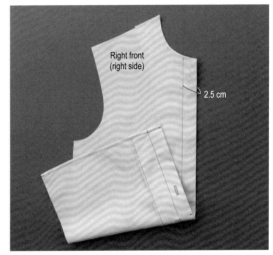

6   Turn the right front facing to the wrong side of the bodice and smooth with the iron, then stitch the front edge. Next, double-fold the seam allowance of the hem and sew. Stitch the front edge after sewing the hem of the facing.

7   Smooth the front edge of the left front bodice and double-fold the hem, then sew. The completed placket.

Sleeve placket and cuff...fabric: broadcloth

Pattern for the sleeve cuff placket

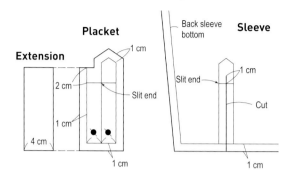

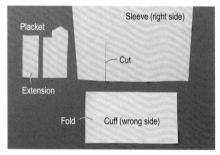

1 Make a mark at the position of the placket at the sleeve, and cut. Attach fusible interfacing on the wrong side of the cuff.

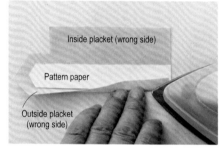

2 Create a pattern paper for the outside placket using paper the same thickness as a postcard. Place the paper on the wrong side of the placket fabric, and fold the seam allowance.

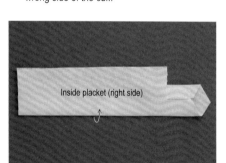

3 While still applying the pattern paper, fold the inside placket back to the outside.

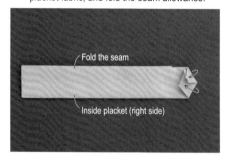

4 Fold the seam allowance of the inside placket, then fold the seam allowance of the triangle part and remove the pattern paper.

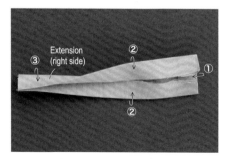

5 With the extension, after folding the upper edge 1 cm, double gate fold to 1 cm in width.

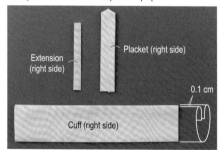

6 For the cuff, fold the seam allowance of the long side, then further fold it in half. Hold the surface cuffs side at around 0.1 cm and smooth with an iron. Each part can be made in advance.

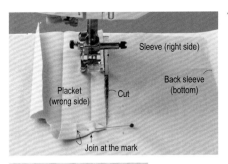

7   At the sleeve placket, fold the outside placket part wrong sides out and sew. The upper edge of the placket is sewn while the seam allowance is folded.

Sleeve (right side)

Placket (wrong side)   Cut   Back sleeve (bottom)

Join at the mark

Sleeve (right side)

Outside placket (wrong side)

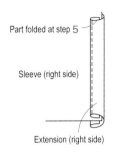

Part folded at step 5

Sleeve (right side)

0.1 cm

Extension (right side)

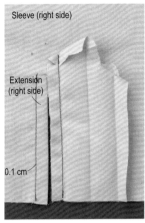

Sleeve (right side)

Extension (right side)

0.1 cm

8   Fold the double gate folded extension over the other side of the cut of the sleeve, and sew.

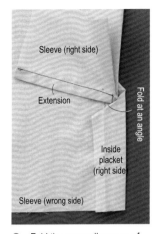

Sleeve (right side)

Extension

Fold at an angle

Inside placket (right side)

Sleeve (wrong side)

9   Fold the seam allowance of the upper edge of the placket into a triangle. Even though you fold the inside placket outward, the upper end of the inside placket is folded at an angle and attached to the extension (cut end).

10   Fold the seam allowance of the end of the inside placket and place a marking pin on the outside placket.

Fold

Sleeve (wrong side)

11   On the extension, overlay the plackets and smooth them out, and place the marking pin where the upper end of the placket fabric is joined with the sleeve.

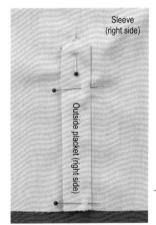

Sleeve (right side)

Outside placket (right side)

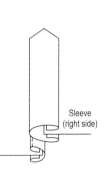

Sleeve (right side)

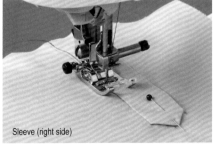

Sleeve (right side)

12   At the placket side, upper edge, and slit end, stitch following the diagram "How to stitch" to the right. The completed sleeve placket.

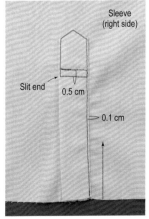

Sleeve (right side)

Slit end   0.5 cm

0.1 cm

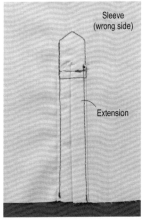

Sleeve (wrong side)

Extension

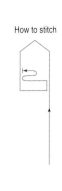

How to stitch

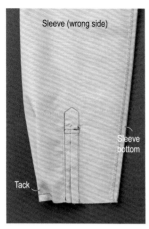

Sleeve (wrong side)

Sleeve bottom

Tack

13 Fold the cuff back and sew the bottom of the sleeve. Overcast stitch (or zigzag stitch) the seam allowance and fold onto the back part.

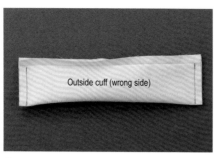

Outside cuff (wrong side)

14 Fold the cuff inside out and sew both edges. At this time, make room on the cuff, by pushing back the edge of the outside cuff part by 0.1–0.2 cm and sew, stopping at the pleat at the top edge.

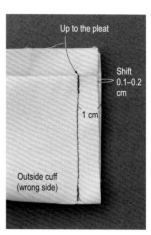

Up to the pleat

Shift 0.1–0.2 cm

1 cm

Outside cuff (wrong side)

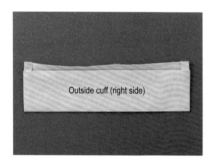

Outside cuff (right side)

15 Return the cuff to the outside, fold the seam allowance on the outside cuff and smooth out the shape.

Inside cuff (wrong side)

Sleeve (wrong side)

16 Join the right side of the inside cuff onto the wrong side of the cuff, and sew while avoiding the outside cuff.

18 Stitch from the right side around the cuff. The seam allowances will overlap, so at the beginning, sew 1–2 cm from the edge back towards it, then change direction and sew along to make it easier.

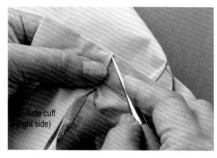

Outside cuff (right side)

17 Turn the seam allowance of the step 16 cuff onto the cuff, covering the right side of the cuff on the seam allowance, and smooth it out. Arrange the ends while pushing down the seam allowance with an awl and fasten with a marking pin.

Outside cuff (right side)

↓

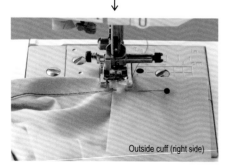

Outside cuff (right side)

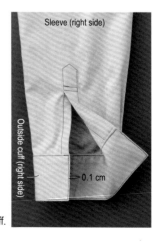

Sleeve (right side)

Outside cuff (right side)

0.1 cm

19 Stitch around the edge of the cuff to complete the cuff.

Slit tailoring
Concealed zipper opening...fabric: wool georgette

Concealed zipper
Make it 2 cm or more longer than the specified size, then sew using the concealed zipper foot.

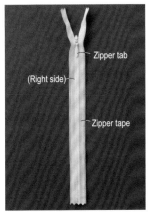
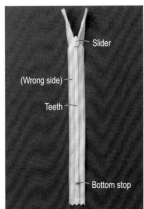

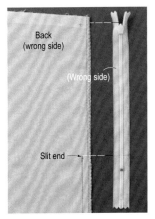

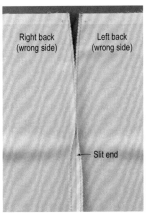
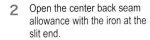

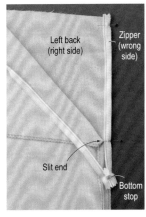

1 Cut the center back of the skirt with a 1 cm seam allowance, then overcast stitch (or zigzag stitch) on the seam allowance. When using thin fabric or other fabric that may be pulled by the zipper, apply adhesive tape on the seam allowance for durability. Match the wrong side of the left and right center back together, and sew from the slit end. Reverse stitch on the slit end firmly. Align the concealed zipper in line with the specified size, and mark the slit end position on the wrong side.

When using thin fabric

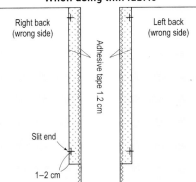

2 Open the center back seam allowance with the iron at the slit end.

3 Move the bottom stop of the zipper to the bottom edge and open the zipper. At the opening of the left center back, overlay the single part of the zipper inside out, join it with the slit end and place a marking pin at the top edge and slit end. Because the zipper tape has a width of 1 cm, match the seam allowance end and the tape end and fasten. While sewing, you can also place a marking pin or use fabric bond (→p. 25) at two or three places between them.

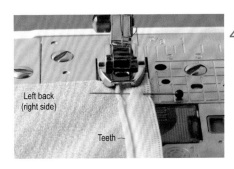

4 Switch the presser foot to the concealed zipper foot, then sew from the top edge toward the slit end. First, insert the teeth of the zipper into the groove on the left side toward the presser foot.

5   Reverse stitch as you start sewing, then raise the teeth with your fingers, and sew while inserting the teeth into the groove of the presser foot.

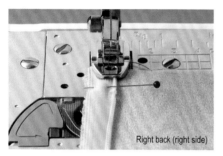

Right back (right side)

7   On the other side of the zipper at the opening of the right center back, place a marking pin like in step 3, insert the teeth into the right grooves going toward the presser foot, and then begin sewing.

6   Sew up to the slit end then reverse stitch.

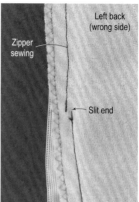

Left back (wrong side)

Zipper sewing

Slit end

↓

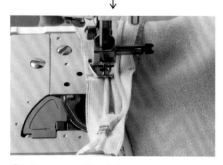

8   As with steps 5 and 6, sew up to the slit end.

Right back (right side)

Left back (wrong side)

9   The zipper sewing will then be finished.

Back (wrong side)

↓

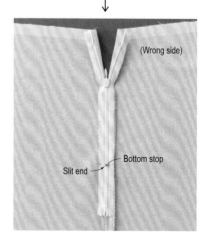

(Wrong side)

Bottom stop

Slit end

10   Take out the tab of the zipper from the slit end, moving the slider upward. Then, move the bottom stop to the slit end.

11 Make sure the bottom stop doesn't move, by tightening it with pliers to keep it fixed into place.

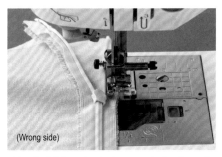

(Wrong side)

13 Switch to a standard presser foot and sew the zipper edge on the seam allowance. At this time, open the zipper about halfway, and sew until you reach the slider.

14 Should the slider get stuck, stop sewing while the needle is still down, raise the presser foot, and pull on the handle. Move the slider behind the presser foot.

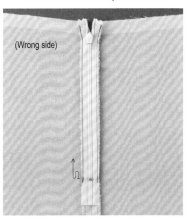

(Wrong side)

16 With the other part of the zipper tape end, while sewing up in the same way, sew from the slit end to the upper edge. The bottom edge of the zipper can also be wrapped in fabric as shown in step 5 on p. 71.

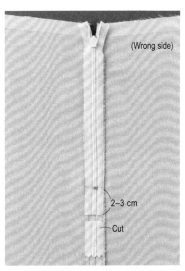

(Wrong side)

2–3 cm

Cut

12 Close the zipper and iron from the outside to make it smooth. The zipper will be longer than needed at the bottom, so cut from 2–3 cm past the slit end.

Slit end

15 Lower the presser foot and continue to sew to the slit end or up to the zipper bottom end.

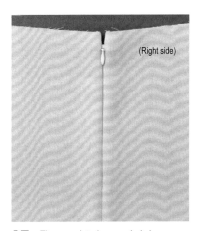

(Right side)

17 The completed concealed zipper. This is the completed version when no lining is used.

Sewing the lining

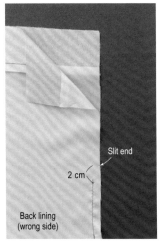

Slit end

2 cm

Back lining
(wrong side)

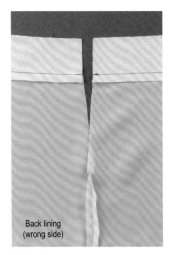

Back lining
(wrong side)

18 For the center back of the
    lining, cut the seam allowance
    at 1 cm, then sew from 2 cm
    below the slit end to the hem.

19 Open the center back seam
    allowance sewn in step 18
    with an iron.

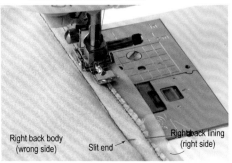

Right back body
(wrong side)   Slit end

Right back lining
(right side)

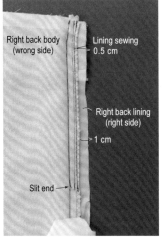

Right back body
(wrong side)

Lining sewing
0.5 cm

Right back lining
(right side)

1 cm

Slit end

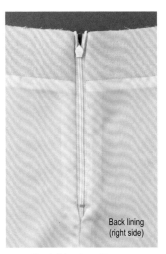

Back lining
(right side)

20 Switch the presser foot to a one-side zipper
    foot. Open the zipper, take the right back lining,
    and at the location of the zipper of the right
    back body, turn them wrong sides out. Push
    back the body seam allowance edge by 1 cm
    from the lining, match the slit ends together,
    and place a marking pin there, then sew up to
    the slit end 0.5 cm on the inside of the body.
    If you have trouble with the zipper slider, see
    steps 14, 15 (→p. 69) to get it to move, and
    then sew.

21 The left back part is sewn same
    as step 20. Sew the surface
    fabric and lining together, move
    them to the outside and smooth
    with an iron.

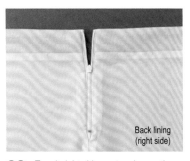

Waist

Back lining
(wrong side)

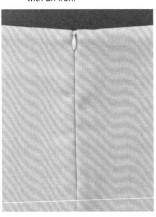

Back lining
(right side)

22 Opening the zipper, turn the body
    and lining of the skirt waists inside
    out for sewing.

23 Turn it right sides out and smooth
    with an iron.

24 The completed zipper.

Slit tailoring
Concealed zipper placket: panel cut lines...fabric: wool georgette

*Sewing method for when thick fabrics form bulky seam allowances where panels meet and cutting is difficult with the concealed zipper foot.
 Use a one-side zipper foot.

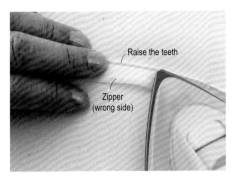

1   Raise the teeth from the wrong side of the zipper and iron.

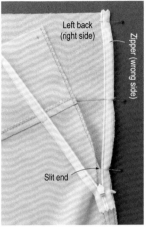

2   Following steps 1 through 3 from p. 67, turn the zipper inside out on the left back skirt and fasten with a marking pin.

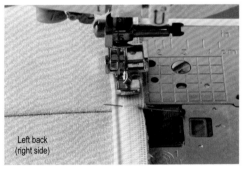

3   Change the sewing presser foot to a one-side zipper foot, sew along the edge of the teeth as the teeth are being raised and sew up to the slit end.

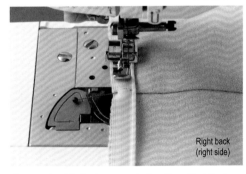

4   For the right back, sew up to the slit end just like in step 3.

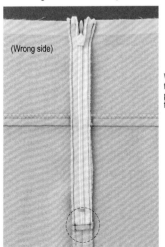

5   Finish by following steps 10–16 on pp. 68–69. For the bottom portion of the zipper tape, you can also wrap it in thin fabric.

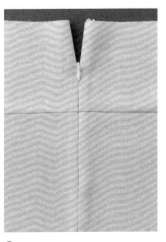

6   The completed zipper.

Zipper opening: side of skirt...fabric: cotton gabardine

The flat knit zipper
A thin, soft zipper used most often in clothing.

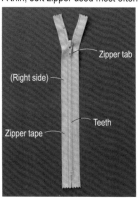

Zipper tab

(Right side)

Teeth

Zipper tape

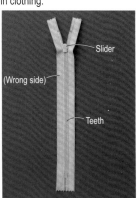

Slider

(Wrong side)

Teeth

[Pattern paper]

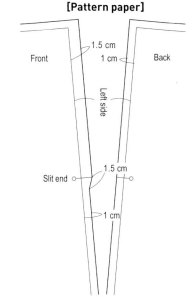

Front

1.5 cm

1 cm

Back

Left side

Slit end

1.5 cm

Slit end

1 cm

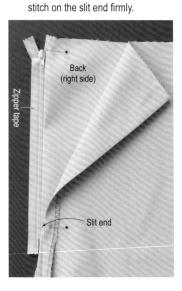

Front
(right side)

Slit end

Back (wrong side)

Back
(right side)

Zipper tape

Slit end

1 Apply adhesive tape with a width of 1.5 cm to the wrong side of the front side opening's seam allowance, and the front and back seam allowances, then overcast stitch (or zigzag stitch).
*When attaching the zipper to the center back, switch from the front to left back, then the back to right back.

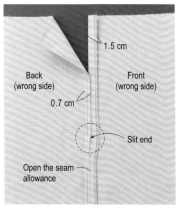

Back
(wrong side)

Adhesive tape

Front
(wrong side)

Slit end

1.5 cm

2 Put the front and back sides together inside out and sew the bottom from the slit end. Reverse stitch on the slit end firmly.

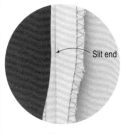

Slit end

1.5 cm

Back
(wrong side)

Front
(wrong side)

0.7 cm

Slit end

Open the seam allowance

3 Open the seam allowance at the bottom from the slit end. Fold the seam allowance at 1.5 cm at the upper front from the slit end, and fold at 0.3 cm from the finish line (0.7 cm) at the back.

4 Overlay the back side at the outside of the zipper, join the side pleats at the teeth, suspending the fabric and place a marking pin. Where the zipper connects to the fabric, it can pucker, so slightly gather the fabric then sew to give a smart finish. This is particularly recommended for thin and soft fabrics.

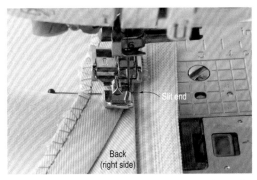
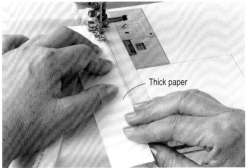

5 Switch the presser foot to the one-side zipper foot and sew the back side pleats. At this time, since you need to sew with the zipper on the right side, move the zipper to the right and sew from the slit end. Sew using paper with the thickness of a postcard so that loose parts are not left out.

6 Stop sewing with the needle down and raise the presser foot. Open the zipper and push the slider behind the foot, then lower the foot and continue sewing.

7 Sew to the upper edge and then reverse stitch.

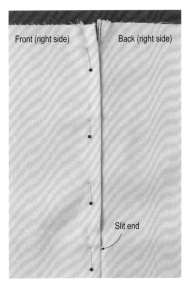

8 Overlap the front sides on the zipper of step 7 and fasten with a marking pin.

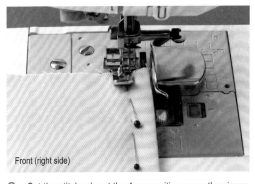

9 Set the stitch ruler at the 1 cm position, open the zipper, and stitch on the front side.

10 Using thick paper, place the pleat on the front side of the stitch ruler and keep sewing.

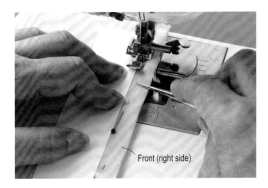

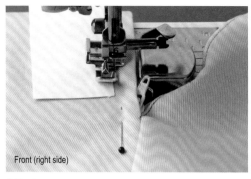

Front (right side)

11 Sew until you cannot go further because of the stitch ruler.

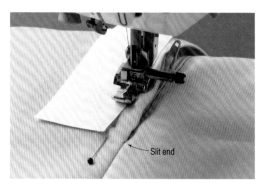

Slit end

12 Remove the stitch ruler and move the slider behind the presser foot as in step 6, and continue sewing.

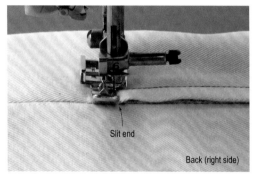

Slit end

Back (right side)

13 When sewing up to the edge of the slit end, raise the presser foot while the needle is down, turn the fabric 90 degrees and change directions. Lower the presser foot and sew up to the slit end, then reverse stitch two to three times.

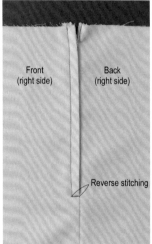

Front (right side)   Back (right side)

Reverse stitching

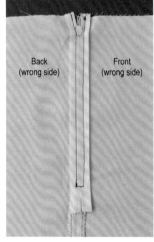

Back (wrong side)   Front (wrong side)

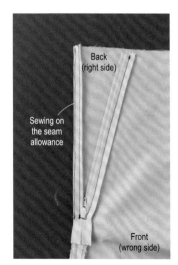

Back (right side)

Sewing on the seam allowance

Front (wrong side)

14 Stop the edge of the back zipper tape at the seam allowance.

15 The completed zipper.

Front zipper opening on pants...fabric: cotton gabardine

Metal zipper

A zipper with metallic teeth. As the metal parts cannot be sewn, purchase a zipper that matches the length of the specified size.

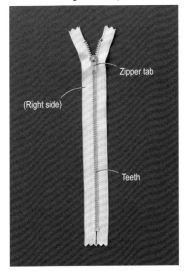

Zipper tab

(Right side)

Teeth

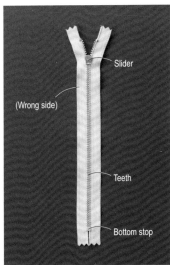

Slider

(Wrong side)

Teeth

Bottom stop

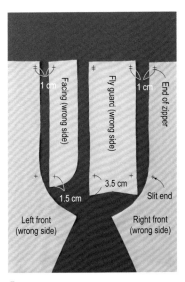

1 cm · Facing (wrong side) · Fly guard (wrong side) · 1 cm · End of zipper

1.5 cm · 3.5 cm · Slit end

Left front (wrong side) · Right front (wrong side)

1 Apply fusible interfacing to the wrong side of the fly guard and the facing.

Fold · Fly guard (wrong side)

1 cm +

2 The fly guard is folded inside out, with the bottom edge sewn at the 1 cm seam allowance.

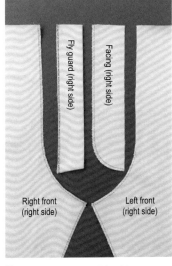

Fly guard (right side) · Facing (right side)

Right front (right side) · Left front (right side)

3 Turn the fly guard right side out, smooth with an iron, and overcast stitch (or zigzag stitch) after sewing on the center front part so that the two pieces won't separate. At the edges of the facing, overcast stitch on the crotch of the pants and the leg bottoms, though only up to around 1 cm of the slit end.

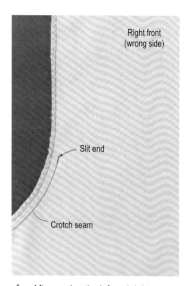

Right front
(wrong side)

Slit end

Crotch seam

4   After sewing the left and right pants
    with the side and crotch of the left
    and right pants, sew up to the slit
    end. Reverse stitch on the slit end.

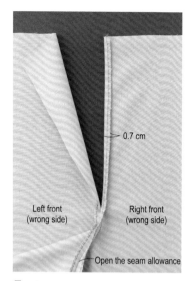

0.7 cm

Left front
(wrong side)

Right front
(wrong side)

Open the seam allowance

5   Open the seam allowance of the
    crotch seam with the iron and fold
    the right front pants to 0.3 cm (0.7
    cm) of the finished seam allowance
    from the end stop.

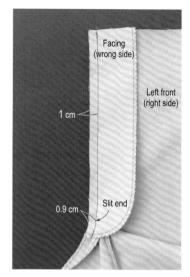

Facing
(wrong side)

1 cm

Left front
(right side)

0.9 cm

Slit end

6   Turn the facings wrong sides out on
    the center front of the left front pants
    and sew. Under the slit end, sew
    slightly into the seam allowance.

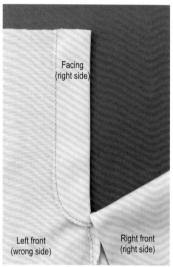

Facing
(right side)

Left front
(wrong side)

Right front
(right side)

7   Return the facing to the wrong side
    of the left front pants, smooth it out
    with an iron while slightly pulling
    back the facing.

Pull back
the facing

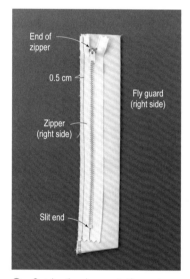

End of
zipper

0.5 cm

Fly guard
(right side)

Zipper
(right side)

Slit end

8   Overlay the zipper onto the center
    front of the fly guard, sewing the
    inside at around 0.5 cm.

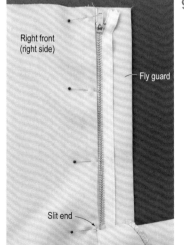

Right front
(right side)

Fly guard

Slit end

9   Overlay the right center
    fronts onto the fly guard
    in step 8, join the pleats
    at the teeth of the zipper
    and place a marking pin.

Thick paper

10 Switch the presser foot to a one-side zipper foot, open
    the zipper and sew the pleats of the right front pants.
    Using paper the thickness of a postcard, stitch while
    pressing with an awl to make sewing easier.

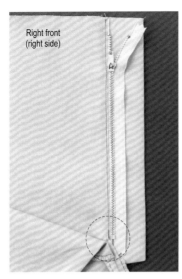

Right front
(right side)

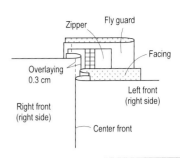

Zipper
Fly guard
Facing
Overlaying
0.3 cm
Left front
(right side)
Right front
(right side)
Center front

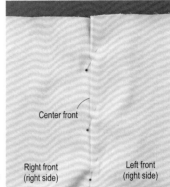

Center front

Right front
(right side)

Left front
(right side)

11 Sew up to the slit end, and if the slider of the zipper gets stuck, move the slider following step 6 on p. 73, then sew.

12 Join the left center front onto the right center front of step 11 and overlay them, then fasten them with marking pins.

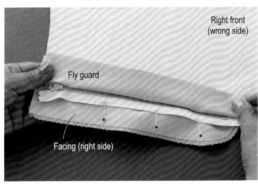

Right front
(wrong side)

Fly guard

Facing (right side)

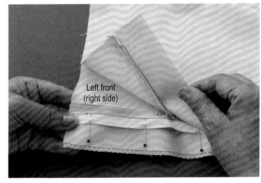

Left front
(right side)

13 Turn over the pieces in step 12 and turn over the fly guard, then place marking pins on the zipper only at the facing. Place them in three to four places from the slit end to 5–6 cm below the waist.

14 Shift the marking pin of the center front of step 12 and open the zipper. For the part at the waist not fastened, smooth it out flat and place a marking pin.

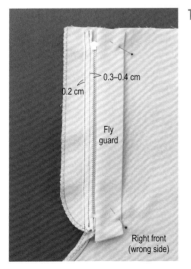

0.3–0.4 cm

0.2 cm

Fly
guard

Right front
(wrong side)

15 Avoiding the fly guard, sew the zipper and facing. Using the one-side zipper foot, first sew the outside part 0.3–0.4 cm of the teeth, then sew the tape side.

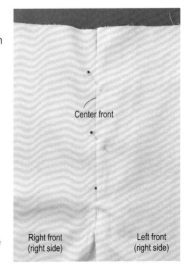

Center front

Right front
(right side)

Left front
(right side)

16 Turn the right side out, join up the center fronts of the left and right again and place marking pins.

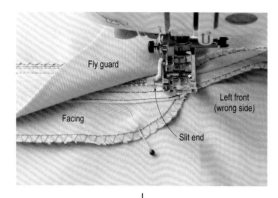

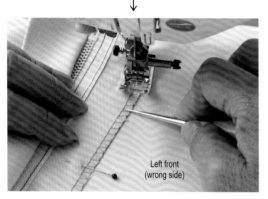

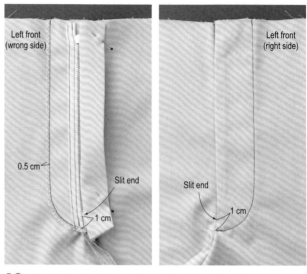

17 Turn it over and sew down 0.5 cm inside of the facing from 1 cm below the slit end while avoiding the fly guard. Reverse stitch at the start.

18 Sew the facing edge up to the waist and sew the facing in place on the left front pants.

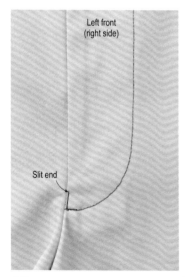

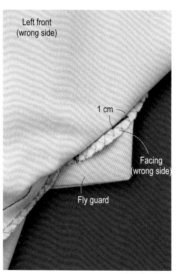

19 Smooth out the fly guard to finish, sew from the slit end to the step 18 stitch two to three times.

20 Turn over the left front pants, lockstitch approximately 1 cm at the stitch curve in step 18 from the wrong side of the facing, then sew the lower end of the facing up to the fly guard.

21 The completed zipper.

Front button placket for pants: lining...fabric: thick wool

*See p. 124 for the pattern

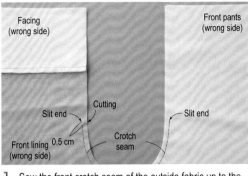

1 Sew the front crotch seam of the outside fabric up to the slit end. For the lining, sew the crotch seams leaving a 0.5 cm gap before the slit end.

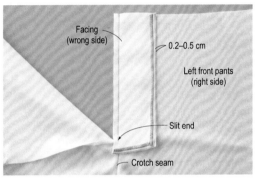

2 Overcast stitch (or zigzag stitch) the edge of the front-opening facing, fold the seam allowance, and stitch that in place. Put the facing and the front edge of the left front pants wrong sides out and sew up to the slit end.

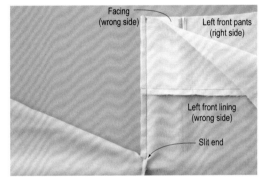

3 Place the left front pants of step 2 and left front lining wrong sides out, then sew up to the slit end like in step 2.

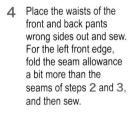

4 Place the waists of the front and back pants wrong sides out and sew. For the left front edge, fold the seam allowance a bit more than the seams of steps 2 and 3, and then sew.

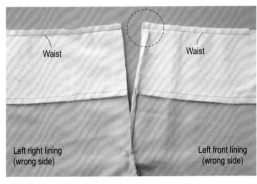

5 Turn the right side out, then iron the waist and left front edge to smooth. For the right front edge, join the edges of the pants and lining, making cuts inside the seam allowance of the crotch end of the pants, then lockstitch at the seam allowance.

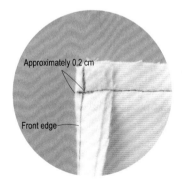

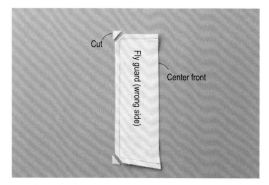

6   Place the fly guards of pants and lining wrong sides out and sew three of the sides, leaving the center front. Cut the seam allowance at an angle.

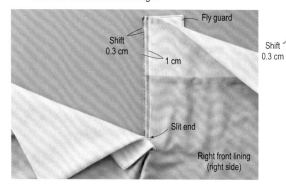

8   Fold the facing under the seam inside out at the right front part, hold the fabric end of the pants at 0.3 cm, and sew up to the slit end at a seam allowance of 1 cm.

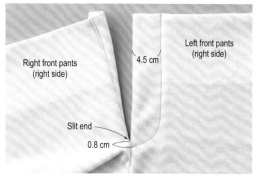

10   Avoiding the right front pants and the facing under the seam, stitch the left front edge.

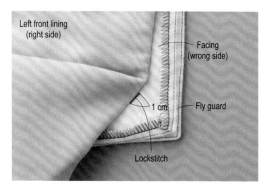

12   Turn over the left front pants, lockstitch approximately 1 cm at the stitch curve of step 10 from the wrong side of the facing, and sew the lower end of the facing up to the fly guard.

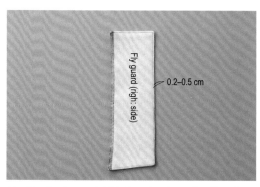

7   Turn the fly guard right side out and smooth with an iron, then stitch. For the center front, overcast stitch both pieces together.

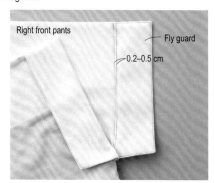

9   Fold the right front edge's seam allowance onto the pants part and smooth it out with an iron, then stitch.

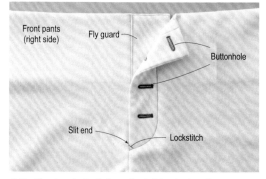

11   Create a buttonhole on the left front edge, then lockstitch at the slit end up to the facing under the seam (two to three reverse stitches).

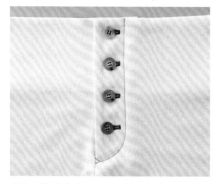

13   Attach the buttons and the placket is completed.

Patch pocket: square...fabric: cotton broadcloth

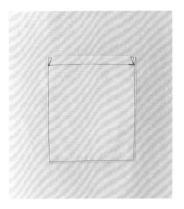

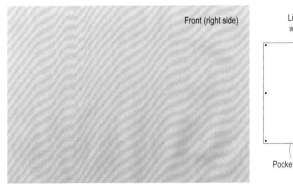

Front (right side)

Lightly mark with an awl

Pocket position

1 Mark the pocket position on the front body by opening small holes with an awl just inside the finish line.

Pocket (right side)

2 Overcast stitch (or zigzag stitch) the seam allowance, but leave the pocket opening.

Fold more

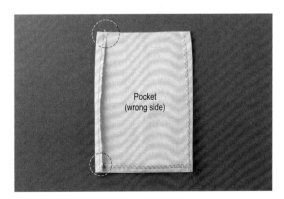

Pocket (wrong side)

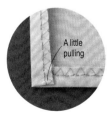

A little pulling

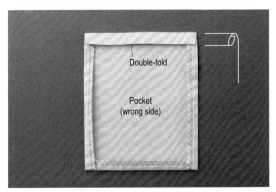

Double-fold

Pocket (wrong side)

4 Double-fold the seam allowance of the pocket hole with the iron.

3 Except for the pocket opening, fold the seam allowance with the iron. Fold at the bottom and both sides. Fold both corners by pulling the seamline on the sides toward the inside without letting the seam allowance to jut out, and adhere them with fabric bond (→p. 25). Fold the corners of the top edge opening a little more inward.

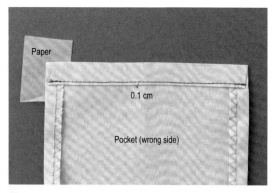

Paper

0.1 cm

Pocket (wrong side)

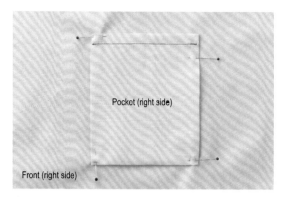

Pocket (right side)

Front (right side)

5   Stitch the opening where it is double-folded. If it's difficult to begin stitching, attach paper (kraft paper or tracing paper) to the bottom and then sew them together so that you can stitch smoothly. Then tear away the paper.

6   Place the pocket in position on the front body and fasten with marking pins.

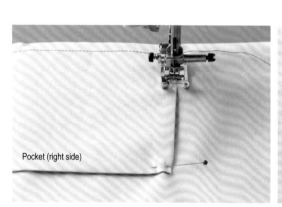

Pocket (right side)

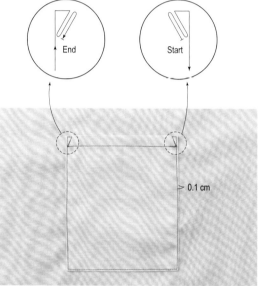

End

Start

0.1 cm

7   Stitch the pocket in place. The pocket opening needs to be reinforced, so stitch a triangle or square (→p. 83 step 5). The completed pocket.

Patch pocket: angled...fabric: cotton broadcloth

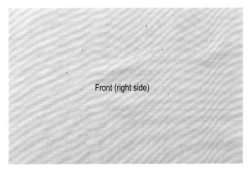

1 Mark the pocket position on the front body by opening small holes with an awl just inside the finish line.

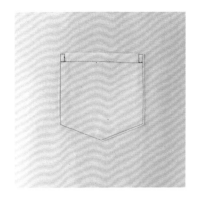

2 Overcast stitch (or zigzag stitch) on the seam allowance, but leave the pocket opening.

Transparent fabric...fabric: cotton lawn

The transparent seam allowance is visible, make the overlapped parts symmetrical when folding at the lower triangle.

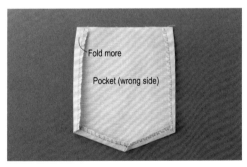

3 Except for the pocket opening, use the iron to fold the seam allowance. Fold the bottom two corners and then both sides, folding at the upper ends a little more to prevent the seam allowance from jutting out.

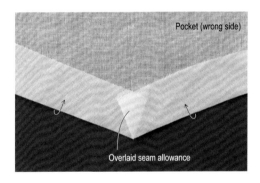

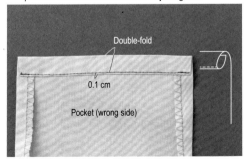

4 Double-fold the seam allowance of the pocket opening and stitch.

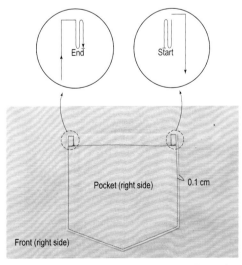

5 Sew the pocket in place on the front body. The pocket opening edges need to be reinforced, so sew a square (→p. 83 step 5) or triangle (→p. 82 step 7). The completed pocket.

Patch pocket: curved...fabric: cotton broadfabric

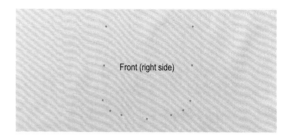

1 Mark the pocket position on the front body by opening small holes with an awl just inside the finish line.

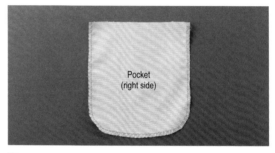

2 Overcast stitch (or zigzag stitch) on the seam allowance, but leave the pocket opening.

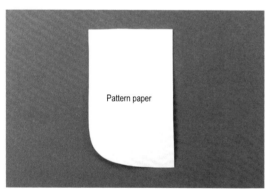

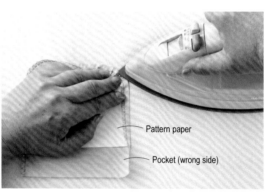

3 Create a pattern paper for the completed pocket using paper the same thickness as a postcard, then attach it on the wrong side of the pocket and fold the seam allowance over with an iron. Smooth out the curves using the tip of the iron while gathering the seam allowance with your fingers.

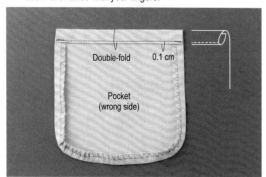

4 Double-fold the seam allowance of the pocket opening, then sew.

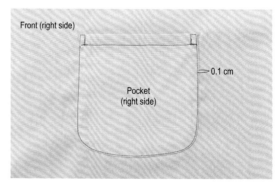

5 The edges of the pocket opening need to be reinforced, so sew a square (→p. 83 step 5) or a triangle (→p. 82 step 7). The completed pocket.

Side seam pocket: French seam and side stitching...fabric: cotton gabardine

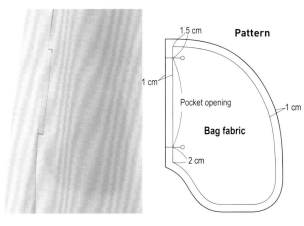

Pattern

1.5 cm

1 cm

Pocket opening

Bag fabric

1 cm

2 cm

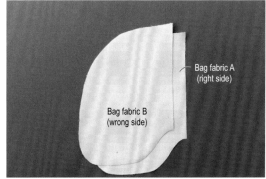

Bag fabric A (right side)

Bag fabric B (wrong side)

1   For the bag fabric, cut pieces for both the inside and the outside. When putting your hand in your pocket, the back of your hand is bag fabric A (connecting to the front body), whereas the palm of your hand is bag fabric B (connecting to the back body).

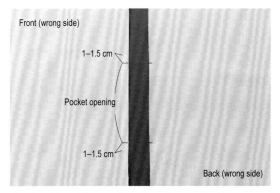

Front (wrong side)

1–1.5 cm

Pocket opening

1–1.5 cm

Back (wrong side)

2   The sides of the body for both the front and back are cut with a 1 cm seam allowance. Use adhesive tape 1.2 cm wide at the seam allowance of the front pocket opening.

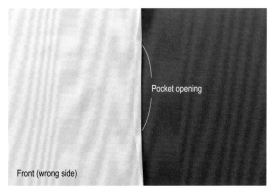

Pocket opening

Front (wrong side)

3   Fold only the seam allowance of the front side's pocket opening with an iron.

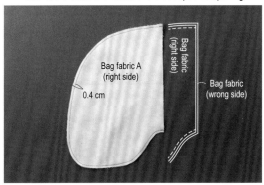

Bag fabric A (right side)

Bag fabric (right side)

Bag fabric (wrong side)

0.4 cm

4   The bag pieces are sewn with a French seam, so first turn the bag parts A and B right sides out, then sew the edge with a seam allowance of 0.4 cm.

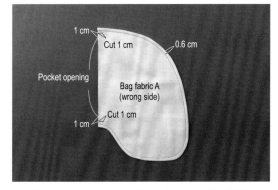

1 cm

Cut 1 cm

0.6 cm

Pocket opening

Bag fabric A (wrong side)

1 cm

Cut 1 cm

5   Turn the bag parts wrong sides out and smooth with the iron, then sew the edge with a seam allowance of 0.6 cm. Next, take only bag fabric and cut 1 cm slits 1 cm from the top and bottom of the pocket opening.

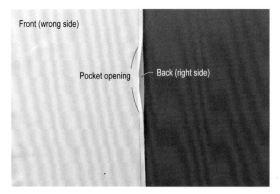

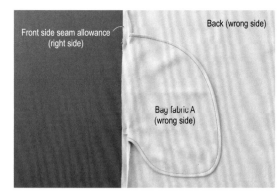

6 Fold the front and back sides wrong sides out, leaving the pocket opening and sew the sides. Reverse stitch at the top and bottom of the pocket opening.

7 On the pocket opening of the front side seam allowance, while avoiding bag fabric B, turn the seam allowance of the pocket opening of bag fabric A inside out, then fasten with marking pins at the top and bottom of the pocket opening from the body front.

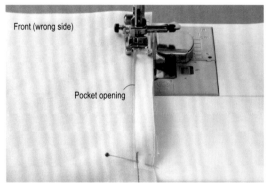

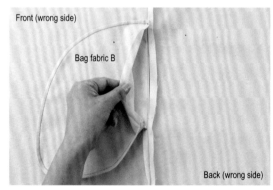

8 Sew the front pocket opening from front body, avoiding the back pocket. At this time, sew at 0.1 cm outside the pleats in step 3.

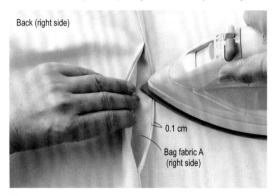

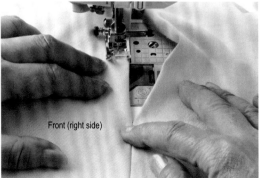

9 Turn right side out, and push the bag fabric A back 0.1 cm, while ironing the front pocket opening.

10 Viewed from the back, sew only the front pocket opening to bag fabric A.

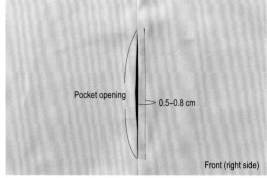

11 From the right side of the front body, stitch the front pocket opening, while avoiding bag fabric B.

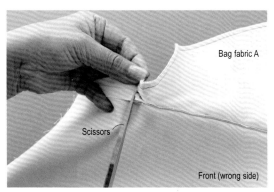

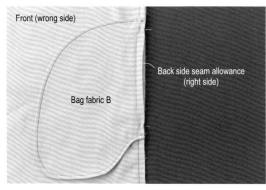

12 Make cuts at the top and bottom of the side seam allowance of pocket opening at the same positions as those on bag fabric A.

13 Place bag fabric B and the seam allowance of the back body wrong sides out, then fasten with a marking pin from the back body side.

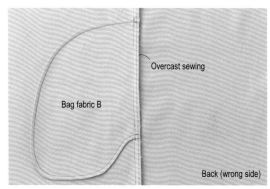

14 Sew the back pocket opening from the back body side. Avoiding the front pocket opening, sew the sides from the top edge of the bag fabric to the bottom edge, sewing slightly outside the French seam along the pocket opening.

15 Overcast stitch both pieces from the seam allowances of the front body, then bring the seam allowance to the back and smooth it out with an iron.

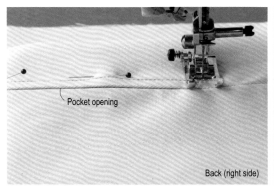

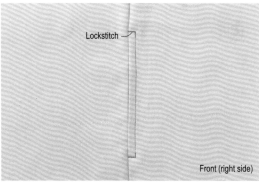

16 Place a marking pin at the pocket opening from the outside of the body, then lockstitch three to four times at the edges of the pocket opening. The completed pocket.

French seam pocket: open side seam...fabric: thick wool

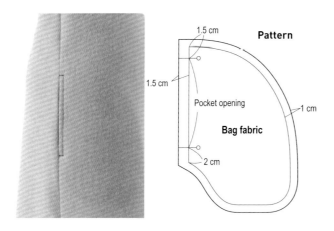

Pattern

1.5 cm

1.5 cm

Pocket opening

Bag fabric

1 cm

2 cm

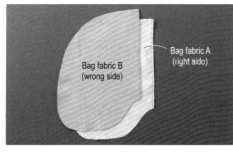

Bag fabric A
(right side)

Bag fabric B
(wrong side)

1. Use a thin cotton (smooth lining) for bag fabric A and use the same outer material for bag fabric B, then overcast stitch (or zigzag stitch) down each French seam. When adding pockets, the back of your hand is bag fabric A (connecting to the front body), whereas the palm of your hand is bag fabric B (connecting to the back body).

2. Cut with a seam allowance of 1.5 cm at both the side of the body and at the front and back. Attach adhesive tape with a 2 cm width onto the seam allowance of the front pocket opening, and overcast stitch the seam allowance on the front and back.

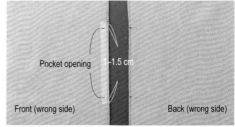

Pocket opening

1–1.5 cm

Front (wrong side)

Back (wrong side)

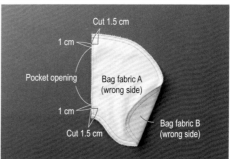

Cut 1.5 cm

1 cm

Pocket opening

Bag fabric A
(wrong side)

1 cm

Cut 1.5 cm

Bag fabric B
(wrong side)

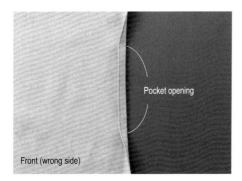

Pocket opening

Front (wrong side)

3. Fold only the seamline of the front side's pocket opening seam allowance with an iron.

4. Fold bag fabric A and B wrong sides out and sew the outer edge, then overcast stitch the seam allowance on both pieces. Next, take only bag fabric A, and at 1 cm from the top and bottom of the pocket opening, cut a slit (1.5 cm) at the finishing line.

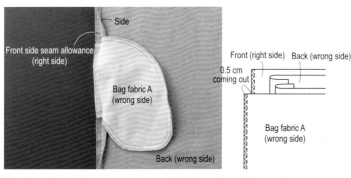

Side

Front side seam allowance
(right side)

Bag fabric A
(wrong side)

Back (wrong side)

Front (right side)   Back (wrong side)

0.5 cm
coming out

Bag fabric A
(wrong side)

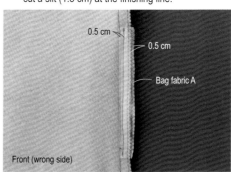

0.5 cm

0.5 cm

Bag fabric A

Front (wrong side)

5. Leave the pocket opening, and sew the front and back sides together (→p. 86 step 6). Next, join the bag fabric A pocket's seam allowances wrong sides out on the pocket opening of the front side seam allowance while avoiding bag fabric B. Push the fabric end of bag fabric A back 0.5 cm and place a marking pin from the front body.

6. Sew the front pocket opening from the front body while avoiding the back pocket opening. Sew the outside fold from step 3 at 0.5 cm.

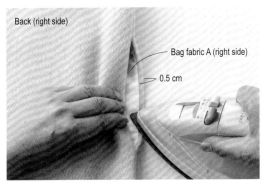

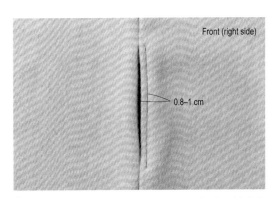

7　Turn right side out and smooth out the front pocket opening while pushing the bag fabric A back 0.5 cm.

8　Stitch the front pocket opening while avoiding bag fabric B (→p. 86 step 11).

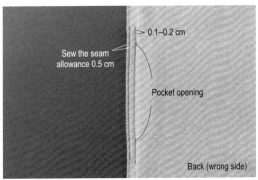

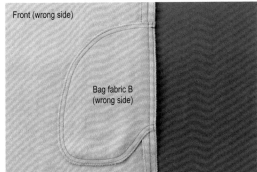

9　Turn bag fabric B and the side seam allowance of the back bodice wrong sides out, then sew the back pocket opening from the back body. Avoiding the front pocket opening, sew slightly outside the side seam at the top and bottom of the pocket opening. Next, sew the ends of the seam allowance.

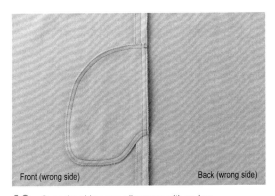

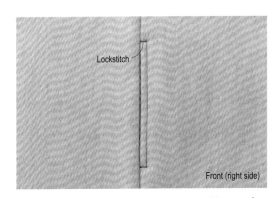

10　Open the side seam allowance with an iron.

11　Lockstitch three to four times at the top and bottom of the pocket opening. The completed pocket.

Piping pocket: one pocket bag...cotton gabardine

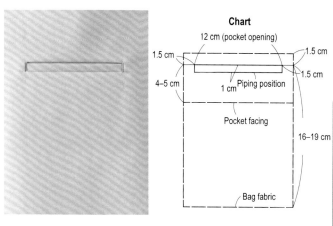

Chart

- 12 cm (pocket opening)
- 1.5 cm
- 1.5 cm
- 1.5 cm
- 4–5 cm
- 1 cm — Piping position
- Pocket facing
- 16–19 cm
- Bag fabric

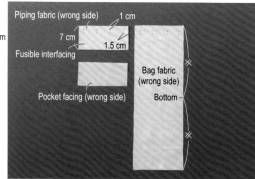

Piping fabric (wrong side) — 1 cm

7 cm — 1.5 cm

Fusible interfacing

Pocket facing (wrong side)

Bag fabric (wrong side)

Bottom

1   For the bag fabric, use fine cotton such as smooth lining, then mark the piping position on one side of the wrong side. Cut the piping fabric and pocket facing fabric using the main fabric, applying fusible interfacing on the piping fabric onto the wrong side and mark the position of the piping. Overcast stitch (or zigzag stitch) the bottom of the pocket facing fabric and piping fabric.

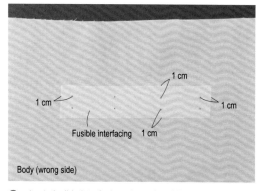

1 cm

1 cm   1 cm   1 cm

Fusible interfacing   1 cm

Body (wrong side)

2   Apply fusible interfacing where the piping will go on the wrong side of the body and mark the piping position.

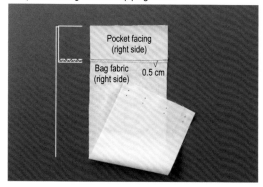

Pocket facing (right side)

Bag fabric (right side)   0.5 cm

3   Overlay the pocket facing fabric on the edge with no marking, on the right side of the bag fabric, then sew the bottom.

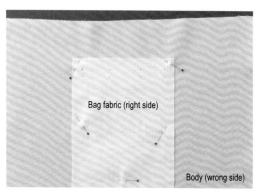

Bag fabric (right side)

Body (wrong side)

4   At the piping position of the wrong side of the body, lay the right side of the bag fabric up and join it with the piping. Fasten it with a marking pin.

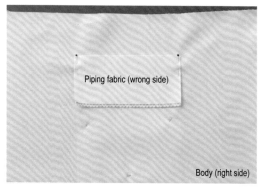

Piping fabric (wrong side)

Body (right side)

5   On the right side of the body in step 4, overlay the piping fabric wrong side out, align where the piping will go and leave marking pins on both sides.

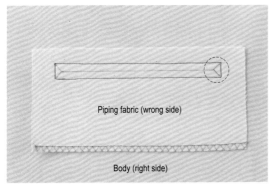

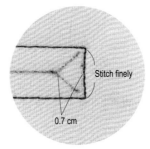

Stitch finely

0.7 cm

6 Sew the piping section. Stitch both edges finely. Next, draw a line for the cut in the center and draw a Y on both ends.

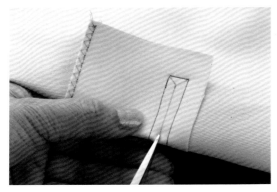

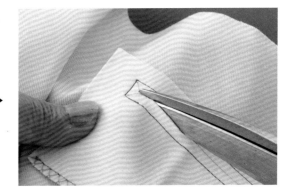

7 Cut along the line in step 6. Cut right to the corners.

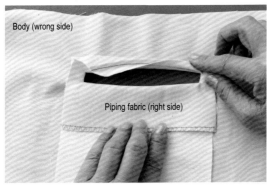

Body (wrong side)

Piping fabric (right side)

8 While cutting, pull the piping fabric onto the wrong side of the body and turn right side out.

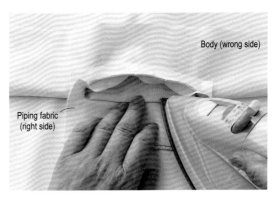

Body (wrong side)

Piping fabric (right side)

9 Turn the seam allowance at the bottom of the piping fabric toward the body and smooth with an iron.

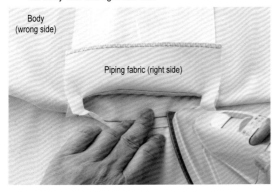

Body (wrong side)

Piping fabric (right side)

10 Turn the seam allowance at the top of the piping fabric toward the body and smooth with an iron.

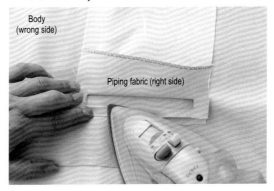

Body (wrong side)

Piping fabric (right side)

11 Smooth out the piping position with the iron to form like a window.

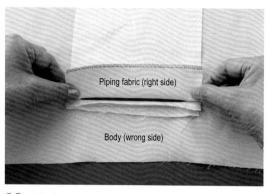 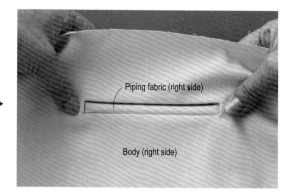

12 Join the piping parts onto the width of the window of step 11 and fold, while holding them in place, then turn the body right side out.

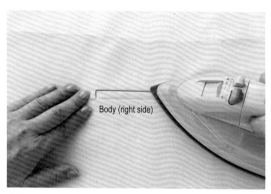 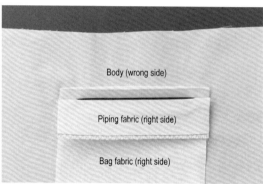

13 Apply the iron on the right side of the body and neaten the piping width.

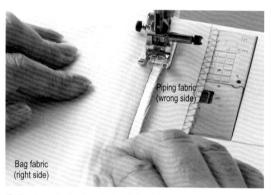 

14 Turn the bottom of the piping fabric, then stitch on the seam at the bottom of the piping fabric to sew the piping fabric.

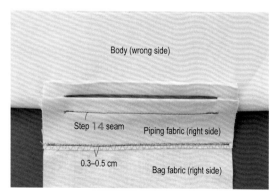 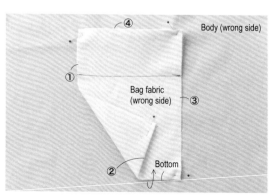

15 Avoiding the body, sew the bottom of the piping fabric to the bag fabric.

16 Fold the bag fabric wrong side out and fasten with a marking pin. Sew around the bag fabric in order from ① to ④.

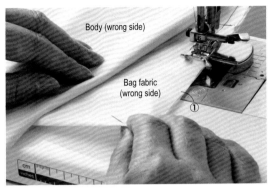

17 Avoiding the bag itself, sew from the bag fabric side touching the body from ① with a 1 cm seam allowance.

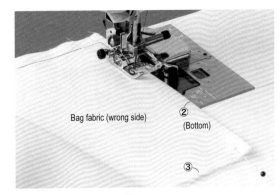

18 Continue sewing to ② (bottom) with a seam allowance of 0.5 cm. The bottom folds over, but, stitch it for stability.

19 Keep sewing to ③ with a 1 cm seam allowance, then to ④ (upper part) with a seam allowance of 0.3 cm.

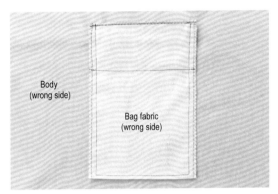

20 Overcast stitch the three points except for the bottom of the bag fabric.

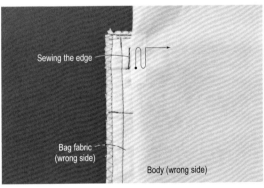

21 Sew the sides of the piping from the bag fabric connected to the wrong side of the body, while avoiding the body.

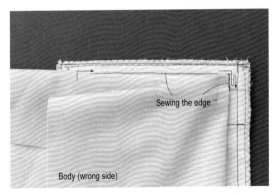

22 Keep sewing from the top edge to the opposite side.

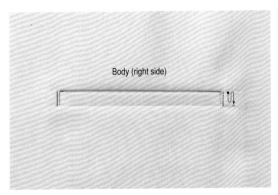

23 Lockstitch three times on each side of the piping on the right side of the body.

Piping pocket: two pocket bags and button fastening...fabric: cotton gabardine

Chart

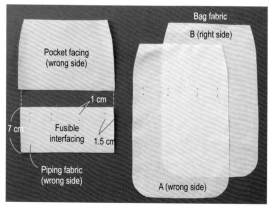

1   Cut two pieces of thin cotton such as smooth lining, and mark the piping position on the wrong side of one of them. Marked bag fabric is A and the unmarked one is B. Cut the piping fabric and the pocket facing fabric using the main fabric, apply fusible interfacing onto the wrong side for the piping, and mark the position of the piping. For both the facing fabric and the piping fabric, overcast stitch (or zigzag stitch) to the bottom.

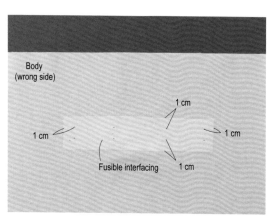

2   Apply fusible interfacing to the piping position on the wrong side of the body and mark the piping position.

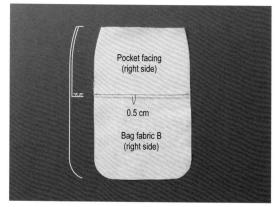

3   Overlay the pocket facing fabric onto bag fabric B and sew the bottom edge.

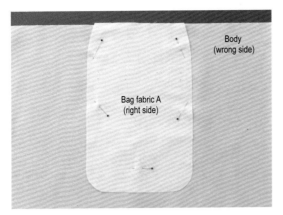

4 Place the bag fabric A right side out on the piping position of the wrong side of the body and join the piping positions for overlaying, then fasten with marking pins.

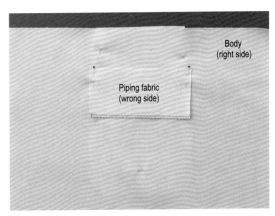

5 Place the piping fabric wrong side out on the right side of the body of step 4, join piping positions and place a marking pin on both sides.

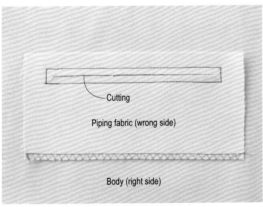

6 Sew the piping in place in the same way as steps 6–7 on p. 91 and cut.

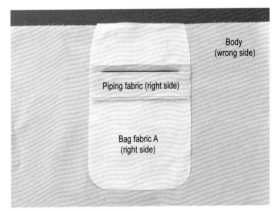

7 Following the same steps 8–13 on p. 91, turn the piping fabric right side out to the wrong side of the body, fold it on the width of the piping, and smooth it out.

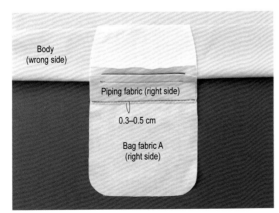

8 As in step 14 on p. 92, sew the lower part of the piping position, avoiding the body, and sew the bottom of the piping fabric onto the bag fabric.

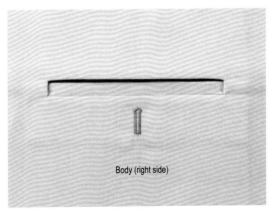

9 Create a buttonhole that goes from the right side through bag fabric A and the piping fabric.

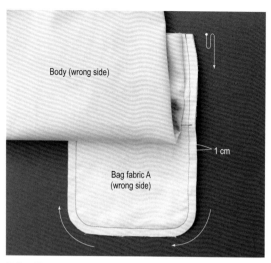

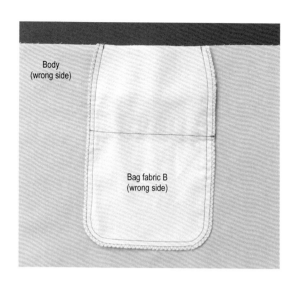

10 Place bag fabric B onto bag fabric A and sew the outer edge from bag fabric A. Next, overcast stitch the seam allowance.

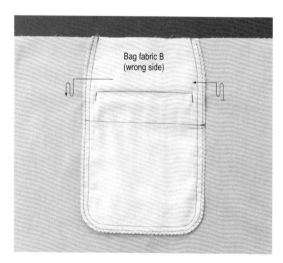

11 Following steps 21–22 on p. 93, sew the inside edge of bag fabric A to the edges of the piping, then to the top edge and the sides.

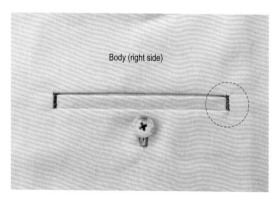

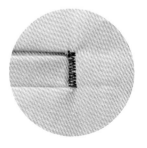

12 From the right side of the body, sew short-width zigzag stitches on both sides of the piping. You can also do this with straight line stitches (→p. 93, step 23). Then cut into the buttonhole (→p. 27), and attach the button to complete the pocket.

Sleeve tailoring
Puff sleeve ...fabric: cotton broadcloth

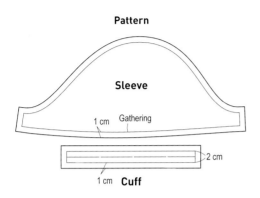

Pattern

Sleeve

1 cm Gathering

2 cm

1 cm **Cuff**

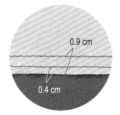

0.9 cm

0.4 cm

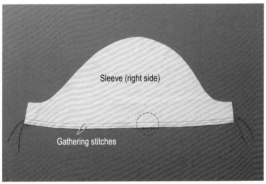

Sleeve (right side)

Gathering stitches

1 Do two lines of baste stitch on the seam allowance of the sleeve to make gathering stitches.

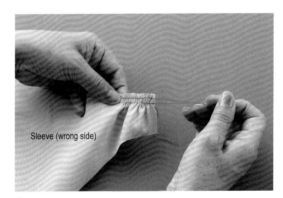

Sleeve (wrong side)

2 Pull the two threads on the wrong side on the sleeve to gather the fabric.

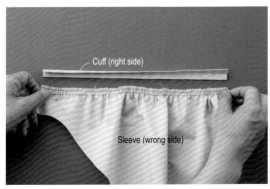

Cuff (right side)

Sleeve (wrong side)

3 Fold the cuff with an iron to the finishing width. For the sleeve gathering, shorten it to the length of the cuff.

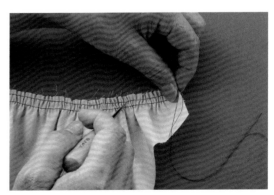

4 Using the tip of the awl, even out the gathering to neaten it.

5 Sleeve with arranged gathering. It is a good idea to slightly shorten the gathered parts near the sleeve bottom.

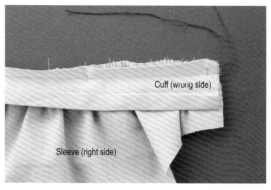

6 Open the fold of the cuff and place on the sleeve opening wrong sides out, then fasten with a marking pin on the sleeve side.

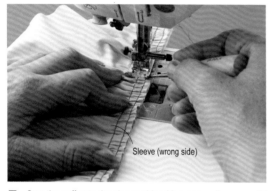

7 Sew the cuff onto the sleeve side with a seam allowance of 1 cm. To make sure that the gathering doesn't twist, sew while pressing down with an awl. Use thick paper alongside, as it will stabilize the gathering and make sewing easier (→p. 99, step 2).

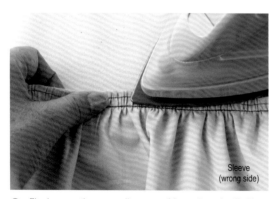

8 Firmly press the seam allowance of the gathered cuff with the iron and push down.

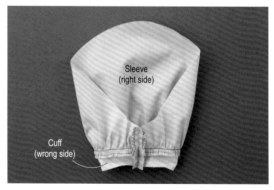

9 Turn the seam allowance connected to the cuff toward the cuff and smooth with the iron. Continue sewing the sleeve bottom to the cuff.

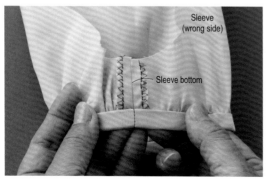

10 Fold the cuff as in step 3 and arrange to the finished width.

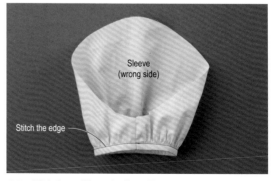

11 Stitch the cuff from the front. The completed sleeve and cuff.

Gathering methods for fabrics that are hard to mark with needles

...fabric: wool georgette

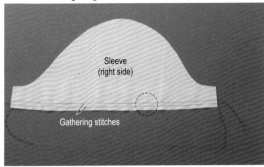 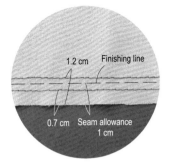

1 Sandwich the finishing line between the cuff and baste stitch the two pieces. When connecting the cuff, stitch between the gathering stitches of the two pieces to give a clean finish with less twisting of the gathering, because the gathering stitches inside the finishing line is removed later. When using fabric with residual needle marks, be sure to do gathering stitches within the seam allowance (→p. 97 step 1).

2 As with steps 2–7 of gather the cuff, folding it wrong side out, then sew. When sewing with the machine, attach paper the thickness of a postcard to press the gathering, as this stabilizes the gathering and makes sewing easier.

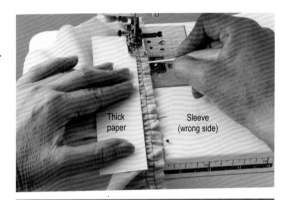

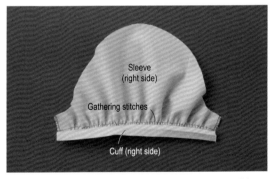 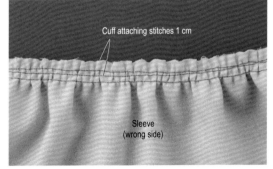

3 Turn the seam allowance connected to the cuff toward the cuff and smooth with the iron. When viewing from the front, you can see one line of the gathering stitches on the cuff.

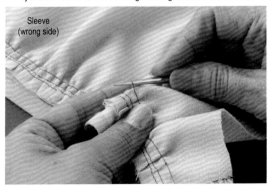 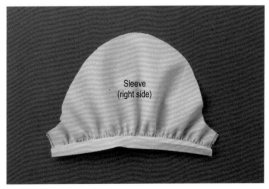

4 Pull out the thread of the upper gathering stitches from the back. To avoid damaging the fabric, remove the yarn by pulling it upward.

5 The completed sleeve and cuff.

Armhole for shirt sleeve...fabric: cotton broadcloth

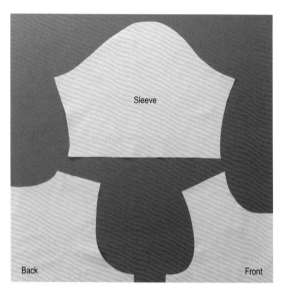

1   Cut the armhole, side of the bodice, the sleeve cap, and
    bottom of the sleeve all with a 1 cm seam allowance.

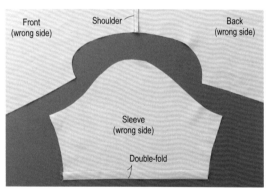

2   Sew the shoulders together for the bodice, double-folding
    the cuff seam allowance of the sleeve.

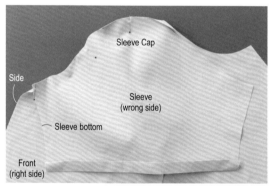

3   Join the sleeves on the sleeve holes of the bodice wrong
    sides out, first placing a marking pin at the halfway point. Put
    marking pins in the areas of the shoulder and sleeve cap, the
    center mark, and the side and sleeve bottom.

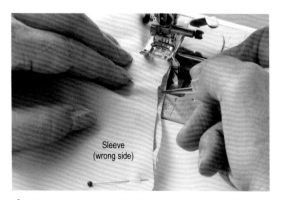

4   Sew from the sleeve side. Use an awl to pull up the bottom
    of the bodice and sew with a 1 cm seam allowance, while
    aligning the two pieces.

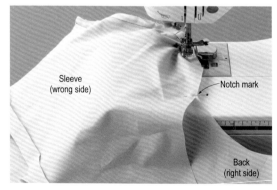

5   Sew up to the shoulder, then stop with the needle down,
    match up the next notch mark and fasten with a marking pin.

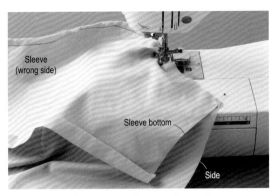

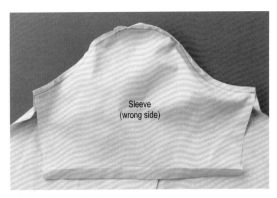

6 As in step 4, continue sewing, and after sewing up to the marking pin in step 5, join the sleeve bottom and side and place a marking pin just like in step 5.

7 Continue sewing the remaining section.

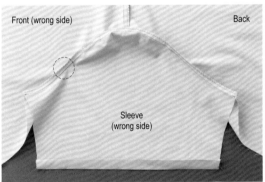

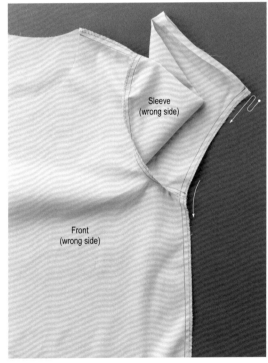

8 On the seam allowance, overcast stitch (or zigzag stitch) both pieces of fabric from the sleeve section, then turn them toward the bodice section and smooth them out with an iron.

9 At the front and back sleeve bottom, turn wrong sides out, then continue to sew from the armhole to the hem. At the seam allowance, overcast stitch both pieces from the front section.

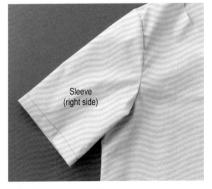

10 Turn the seam allowance of the sleeve bottom to the side toward the back and smooth with an iron, then double-fold the cuff and stitch.

11 The completed sleeve.

Armhole for shirt sleeve: flat-felled seam...fabric: cotton lawn

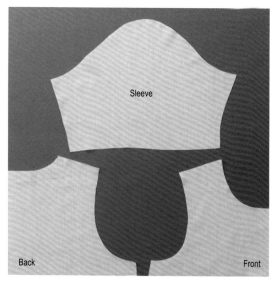

1   Cut the armhole, side of the bodice, the sleeve cap, and
    bottom of the sleeve all with a 1.5–2 cm seam allowance.

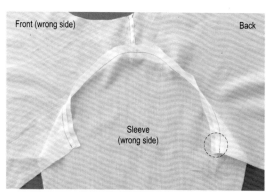

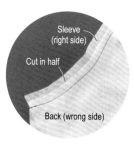

2   Sew the flat-felled seam of the shoulder (→p. 16), turning
    the bodice and sleeve wrong sides out, and as in steps 3–7
    on pp. 100–101, sew at a seam allowance of 1.5–2 cm.
    Next, cut the seam allowance of the bodice in half.

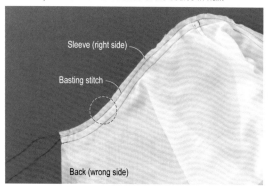

3   For the wide arm-sleeve seam allowance (the sleeve), do
    basting stitch. Machine stitch the seam allowance of the
    narrow sleeve part (the bodice).

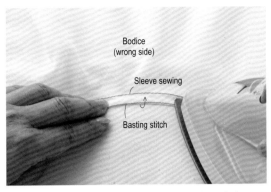

Bodice (wrong side)

Sleeve sewing

Basting stitch

4   For the curved part near the bottom of the sleeve-hole seam allowance, fold the wide sleeve seam allowance with an iron along the basting stitch.

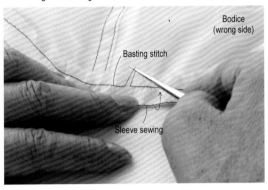

Bodice (wrong side)

Basting stitch

Sleeve sewing

6   For the seam allowance on the curve of the sleeve cap, fold it toward the bodice along the sleeve stitching. Pull the basting stitch thread with an awl, placing it with the curve of the sleeve cap and shorten the seam allowance.

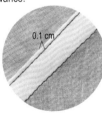

0.1 cm

8   Turn the folded arm-sleeve seam allowance toward the bodice and iron to smooth it out, then do stitching on the edge of the seam allowance. Remove the basting stitch thread.

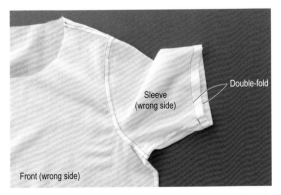

Sleeve (wrong side)

Double-fold

Front (wrong side)

9   Continue sewing the front and back sleeve bottom side with the flat-felled seam, then double-fold the seam allowance of the sleeve hole and stitch it.

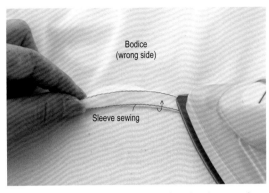

Bodice (wrong side)

Sleeve sewing

5   Fold the seam allowance in step 4 from the sleeve sewing toward the bodice section.

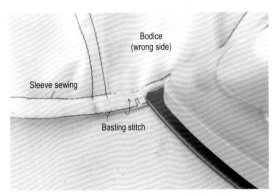

Bodice (wrong side)

Sleeve sewing

Basting stitch

7   Fold the decreased seam allowance onto the bodice alongside the basting stitch and smooth it out with an iron.

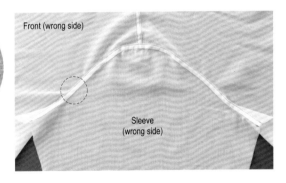

Front (wrong side)

Sleeve (wrong side)

Sleeve (right side)

10   The completed sleeve.

Armhole for shirt sleeve: French seam...fabric: chiffon georgette

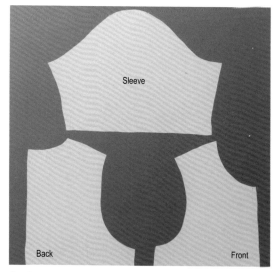

1   Cut the sleeve hole, side of the bodice, the sleeve cap, and sleeve bottom all with a seam allowance of 1 cm.

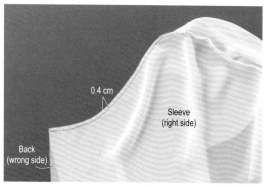

2   Sew the shoulder of the bodice with a French seam (→ p. 16). Align the bodice and sleeves right side out, and following steps 3–7 on pp. 100–101, sew with a 0.4 cm seam allowance.

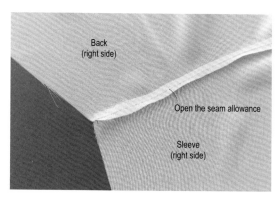

3   Open the two seam allowances using an iron.

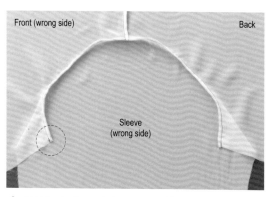

4   Fold the bodice and sleeve wrong sides out and sew at a seam allowance of 0.6 cm. Turn the seam allowance toward the sleeve part and smooth out with an iron.

5   Sew a French seam from the sleeve underside to the bodice side, double-fold the seam allowance of the cuff, and stitch to complete the sleeve.

Armhole with set-in sleeve: shirring...fabric: wool georgette

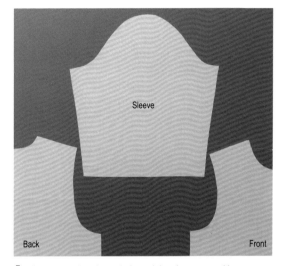

1 Cut the bodice sleeve hole and the sleeve cap with a seam allowance of 1 cm.

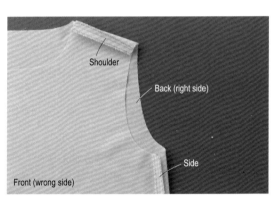

2 Sew the shoulder and sides of the bodice.

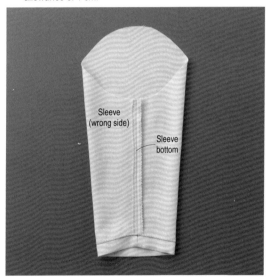

3 Sew the sleeve and sleeve bottom to finish the sleeve opening.

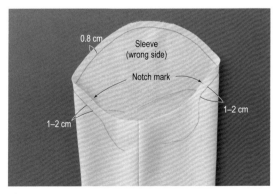

4 Do basting stitch on the seam allowance of the sleeve cap to add slack. Make sure to have the notch mark at both the front and back be within 1–2 cm of the sleeve bottom.

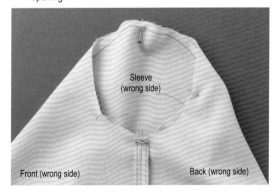

5 Fold the sleeves wrong sides out at the sleeve hole of the bodice, join the shoulder and sleeve cap, the front, and back notch marks, then fasten a marking pin from the sleeve section.

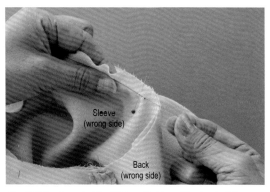

6 Pull the thread of the thicker stitching at the back of the wrong side of the sleeve to shorten it.

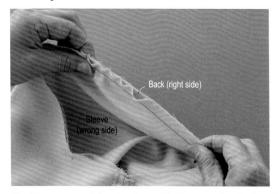

8 Repeat steps 6–7 a few times. Join the sleeve lengths from the shoulder to the notch mark with the bodice. Distribute the slack a bit more on the sleeve cap while making sure that it doesn't gather.

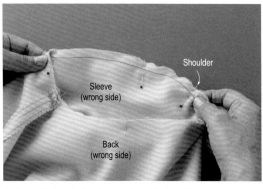

10 Add slack to the front part and fasten with a marking pin.

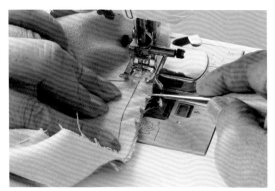

12 For the part with slack, sew while pressing on the slack with an awl, then sew around the armhole. After sewing, overlay stitches 5–6 cm at the starting seam.

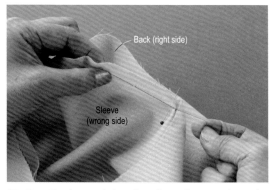

7 Draw the shortened piece through your fingers and move it to the sleeve cap.

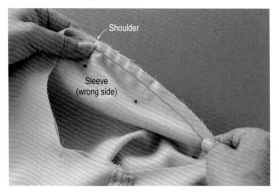

9 Place a marking pin in the center of the slack part.

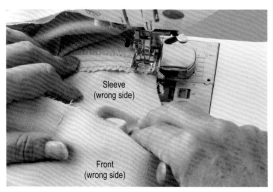

11 Sew the armhole from the sleeve side. Begin sewing from the sleeve bottom and keep sewing while joining the bodice and edge of the sleeves.

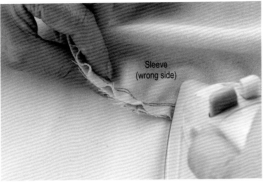

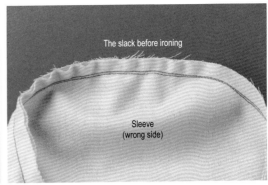

13 To make sure the seam allowance of the slack part doesn't puff out, firmly press the seam allowance with the iron.

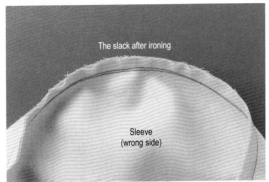

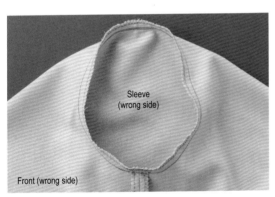

14 Overcast stitch (or zigzag stitch) on both the pieces together on the sleeve hole seam allowance.

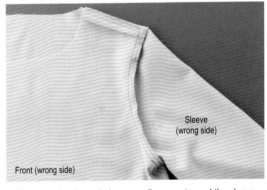

15 Turn the sleeve hole seam allowance toward the sleeve part and smooth with an iron.

16 The completed sleeve.

Folding methods for pleats...fabric: cotton broadcloth

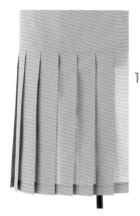

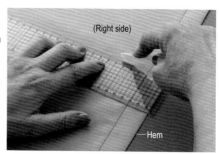

(Right side)

—Hem

1 Set the skirt hem up to be finished. Mark the location of both the exterior pleat top and the shadow fold on the exterior surface of the fabric. When inserting seams, determine the position the seam will come from at the shadow fold. For smooth fabrics that are difficult to mark, use chalk or a marking pen on the wrong side of the fabric.

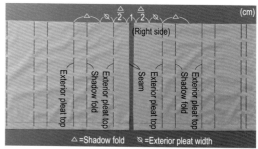

(cm)

(Right side)

△ =Shadow fold ◎ =Exterior pleat width

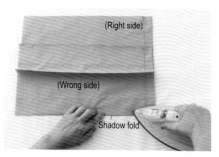

(Right side)

(Wrong side)

Shadow fold

2 Fold the shadow fold inside out with the iron. From the ends, fold all the shadow folds in order.

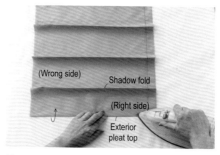

(Wrong side)

Shadow fold

(Right side)

Exterior pleat top

3 Fold the exterior pleat top with an iron inside out. From the ends, fold all the exterior pleat tops in order.

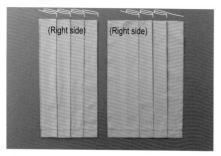

(Right side) (Right side)

4 Arrange the pleats on the fold peak.

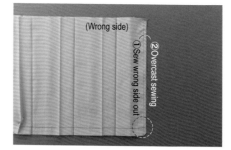

(Wrong side)

①Sew wrong side out

②Overcast sewing

5 For the pieces, turn the seam position wrong sides out and sew. For the seam allowance, overcast stitch (or zigzag stitch) on the two pieces of fabric, then fold the seam allowance edge to sew the hem.

Fold

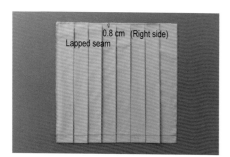

0.8 cm (Right side)

Lapped seam

6 Arrange the pleats and machine stitch the top edge seam allowance.

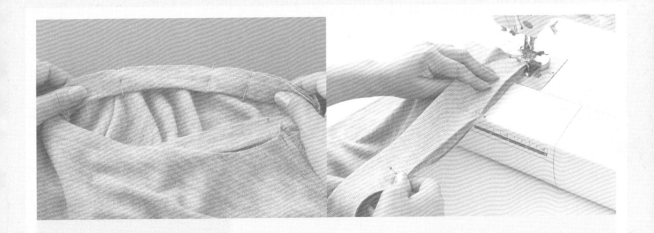

KNIT FABRIC
TAILORING

Basics for sewing knitted fabric

Sewing machine thread for knit fabric

Sewing machine needle for knit fabric

Typical knit fabric

Jersey knit: Plain stitching. The appearance of the stitching on the surface and inside will be different. Its feature is a cut end that easily curls.
Rib-knit: Rib stitch. The stitching on the outside and inside look like ribs. It stretches horizontally.
Double knit: Double-sided knitting. Knitted area of double rib-knit. Its feature is it has a higher density and is thicker than rib-knit.

Thread and needle

● To sew stretchy knit fabric, use a sewing thread (such as Resilon) so the stitching can match the stretching of the fabric.

● So that the knit fabric isn't damaged by the needle end, use a sewing needle for knit fabric that is rounder than a normal needle.

Points for sewing

● For the sewing needles, use normal to slightly large ones. Take care when using thin needles, as they pull the fabric more easily.

● When sewing with the machine, place the fabric in a flat, natural position, then sew while making sure not to pull on it. When sewing in a horizontal direction, where pulling easily occurs, use thick paper to stop pulling.
  →**Hemming**

● It is easy for waviness to occur with the seam when sewing with knit fabric, so when you have finished sewing, make sure to iron the seam to reduce this effect.

Dealing with the seam allowance

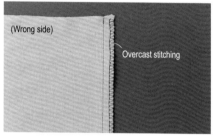
(Wrong side)
Overcast stitching

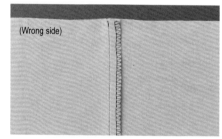
(Wrong side)

1   Align the two pieces wrong sides out and sew. For the seam allowance, overcast stitch (or zigzag stitch) the two pieces and smooth with an iron. This method is the most suitable, but not for thick knit fabric.

2   Turn the seam allowance over to one side and iron.

Hemming

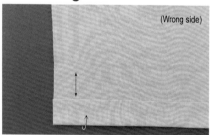
(Wrong side)

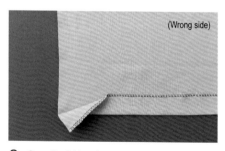
(Wrong side)

1   Fold the hem seam allowance to the wrong side with the iron. To fold accurately, it is best to fold before overcast stitching.

2   Open the fold and overcast stitch on the edges of the hem seam allowance.

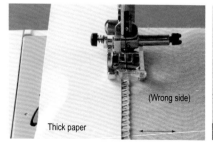
(Wrong side)
Thick paper

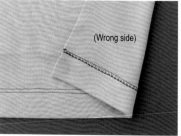
(Wrong side)

3   Fold over the fold in step 1 and stitch the seam allowance edge. In order to sew in a horizontal direction, because stretching occurs easily, try using paper the thickness of a postcard when sewing. While one stitch is enough, using two stitches makes the seam allowance more stable.

Sewing the shoulder

When the shoulder seam is stretched, the silhouette of the clothing is ruined.
To prevent this stretching, you can apply adhesive tape or general fabric tape when sewing.

Apply adhesive tape

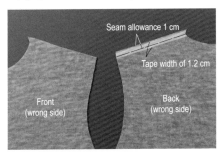

1 On the wrong side of the shoulder seam allowance from the back, fasten adhesive tape so that it attaches to the sewing line. Use adhesive tape for knit fabric.

Using general fabric tape

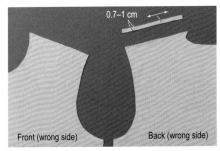

1 Cut the anti-stretch tape to run vertically on the garment fabric with a width of 0.7–1 cm and the same length as the shoulder or slightly longer.

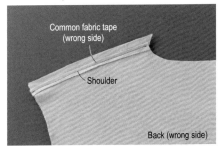

2 Place the front and back bodice shoulders wrong sides out, then sew them together while overlaying common fabric tape on the back shoulder.

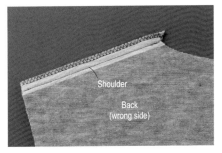

2 Join the shoulders of the front and back bodice wrong sides out, then overcast stitch on the two pieces of fabric from the front bodice at the seam allowance.

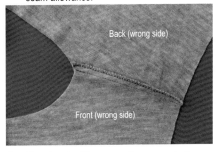

3 Turn the shoulder seam allowance onto the back side and smooth with an iron.

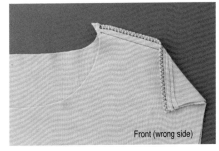

3 On the seam allowance of the shoulder, overcast stitch from the side of the front bodice. Turn the seam allowance to the back and smooth out with an iron.

In the event the cut edge curls...
A good way to handle cut edges curling on jersey knit is to use spray adhesive (→p. 15). Lightly spray the adhesive onto the cut edge and iron only, and the fabric end will come loose for easier sewing.

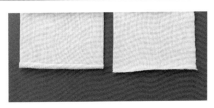

Left: The cut knit fabric with curled edges.

Right: Knit fabric that has been sprayed and ironed.

Knit fabric round neck: common fabric tape...fabric: double knit

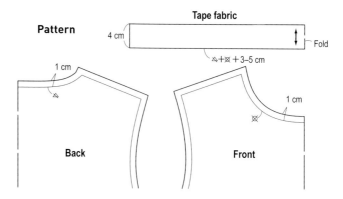

Pattern

Tape fabric

4 cm

Fold

△ + ⊠ + 3–5 cm

1 cm

1 cm

Back

Front

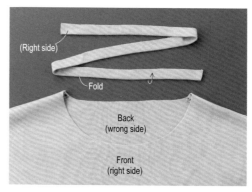

(Right side)

Fold

Back
(wrong side)

Front
(right side)

1 The tape fabric is cut to run vertical to the garment fabric, with a width of 4 cm and cut 5–10 cm longer than the specified neckline, then folded twice with an iron on the wrong side. Cut the bodice with a seam allowance of 1 cm at the neckline, and join it with the shoulder.

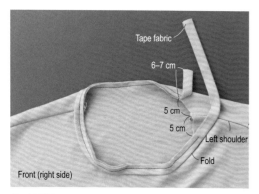

Tape fabric

6–7 cm

5 cm

5 cm

Left shoulder

Fold

Front (right side)

2 Fold the tape fabric onto the neckline of the bodice wrong sides out, then sew the neckline from the left shoulder leaving 5 cm at the front and back edges.

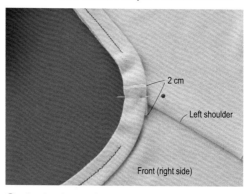

2 cm

Left shoulder

Front (right side)

3 Overlay the tape fabric edge at the left shoulders by 2 cm and cut the excess.

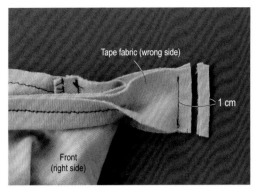

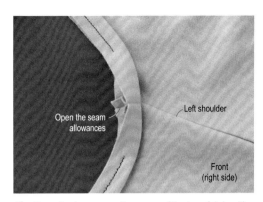

4   Turn the edges of the front and back tape pieces wrong sides out, sew at a seam allowance of 1 cm, then cut the seam allowance almost in half.

5   Open the four seam allowances of the tape fabric with an iron.

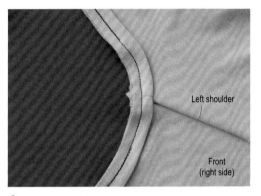

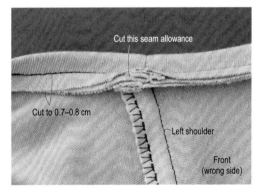

6   Take the folded tape fabric and fold it once more, then add it to the neckline and sew the remaining neckline.

7   Cut the seam allowance of the neckline to 0.7–0.8 cm. For the left shoulder, the seam allowances of the various pieces overlap, so create a difference by cutting to avoid bulkiness.

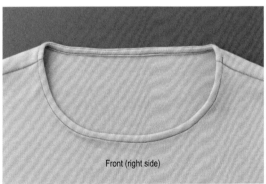

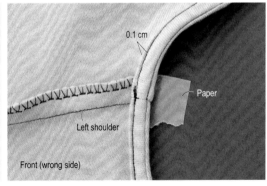

8   Turn the tape fabric toward the wrong side of the bodice, hold the tape fabric and iron the neckline, then stitch. With the left shoulder, if you find it difficult to sew due to the overlapping seam allowances, use thin paper (like kraft paper or tracing paper) at the bottom of the bodice, and sew them together to make stitching easier. Tear away the paper later. The completed neckline.

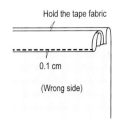

Knit fabric round neck: adding neckline fabric...fabric: jersey knit

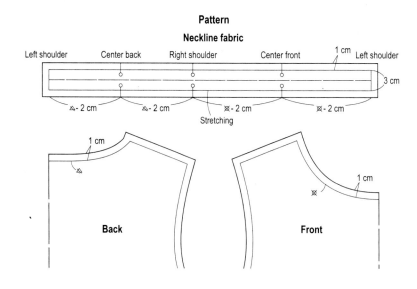

Pattern

Neckline fabric

Left shoulder   Center back   Right shoulder   Center front   1 cm   Left shoulder

3 cm

⊿- 2 cm   ⊿- 2 cm   ⊠- 2 cm   ⊠- 2 cm

Stretching

1 cm

⊿

Back

1 cm

⊠

Front

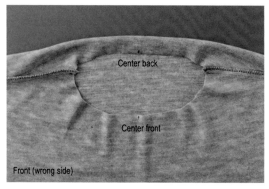

1   Sew the shoulder of the bodice and create a mark at the front and center back on the wrong side of the neckline.

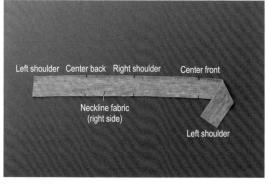

2   For the neckline fabric, add a notch mark on the right shoulder at the center front and back on the right side.

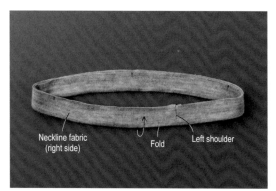

3   Sew together the left shoulder of the neckline fabric and make it into a loop, folding in half from the inside and smoothing it out with an iron.

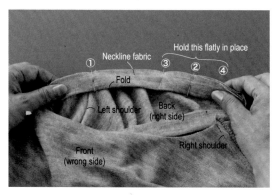

4   At the neckline of the bodice, join the pieces of neckline fabric wrong sides out, adding notch marks to them and fastening with marking pins. First is the left shoulder (①), then the center back (②), and the areas where curve of the left and right neckline of the center back begins (③, ④). For ②–③ and ②–④, join the neckline fabric and bodice flat, then place marking pins. Fasten the right shoulder and the front neckline with marking pins too.

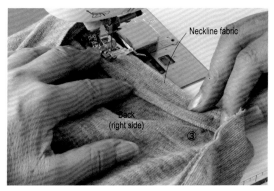

5   Move the neckline up and begin sewing from the left shoulder. From the left shoulder (①) to the marking pin in ③, join onto the bodice, stretching the neckline fabric as you sew.

6   ③–②–④ are joined flat, so sew them without stretching the fabric.

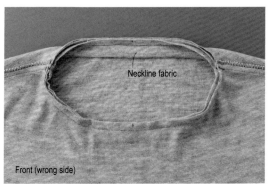
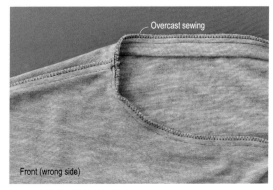

7   Sew the remaining neckline just like in steps 5 and 6, round in a circle.

8   From the neckline fabric side, overcast stitch (or zigzag stitch) the three pieces together on the seam allowance.

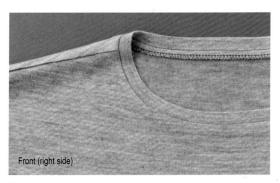

9   Turn the neckline seam allowance toward the bodice side and smooth with the iron.

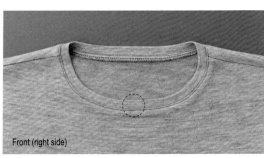

10 For the neckline seam, stitch the seam allowance onto the bodice. The completed neckline.

Attaching rib-knit to the hem...fabric: jersey knit and rib-knit

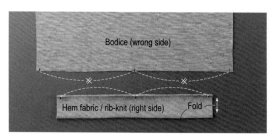

1   Fold the rib-knit to be connected to the hem toward the inside and smooth with the iron. Even out the bottom edge of the bodice and the rib-knit and add notch marks. Here one mark is shown in the center, but if the fabric is longer, you can add two or three equally distanced marks.

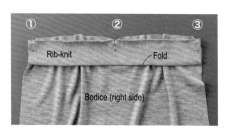

2   Turn the rib-knit and the bodice wrong sides out, join the notch marks and place a marking pin at that point.

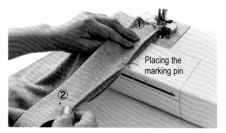

3   Sew from the rib-knit section. When starting to sew, reverse stitch around 1 cm, then stop with the needle down. Hold the position of the central marking pin (②), stretch the rib-knit until the bodice becomes flat, then place a marking pin in the center.

4   Overcast stitch the seam allowance for the three pieces (or zigzag stitch). Sew while stretching the rib-knit.

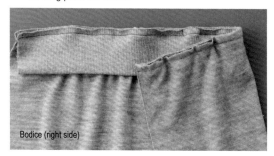

5   Sew ②–③ as shown in steps 3 and 4.

6   Overcast stitch (or zigzag stitch) on the seam allowance for the three pieces. Sew while stretching the rib-knit.

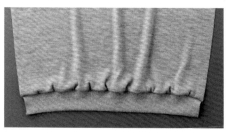

7   Turn it back to the right side to finish. Even if you don't use an iron, the seam allowance will naturally fold toward the bodice section.

TAILORING CLOTHING

Gathered blouse

Size
Bust 156 cm, Length 67.2 cm
*Corresponding full bust size: 82–90 cm

Material
Main fabric (cotton lawn lace) … 110 cm width, 160 cm
Other fabric (cotton lawn) … 110 cm width, 160 cm
Fusible interfacing … 90 cm width, 70 cm
Buttons … Diameter 1.2 cm, 7 pcs

Steps
*Put fusible interfacing on the wrong side of the front edge facing, the collar stand, and the outer upper collar.

1 Attach the facing to the front edge.
   ❶ Match the right sides of the front edge of the front bodice and the facing, and sew.
   ❷ With the facing turned to the wrong side of the bodice, fold over the seam allowance of the facing edge, smooth it with an iron, and sew.

2 Sew the bodice and yoke together.
   ❶ Gather the top edges of the front and back bodice.
   →For how to gather, see p. 97
   ❷ Sandwich the back bodice between the inner and outer yokes, and sew.
   ❸ Match the right sides of the front bodice and the outer yoke, and sew.
   ❹ Fold the seam allowance of the front edge of the inner yoke, and sew up the front and back edges of the yoke.

3 Make and affix a shirt collar with a collar stand.
   →See p. 53

4 Sew back the sleeve hole with bias tape. →See p. 35

5 Sew the sides. Overcast stitch (or zigzag stitch) the two seam allowances together, and fold backward.
   →See p. 16

6 The hem seam allowance is double-folded and stitched.

7 Make buttonholes (→see p. 27) and attach buttons.

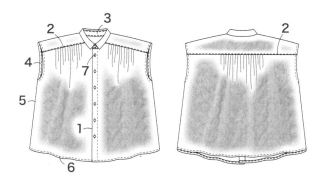

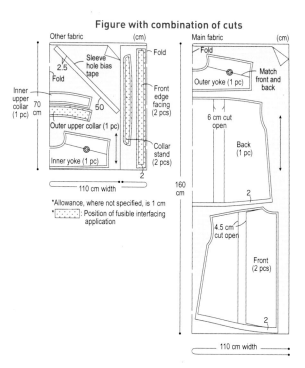

Figure with combination of cuts

*Allowance, where not specified, is 1 cm
⬚ : Position of fusible interfacing application

Pattern

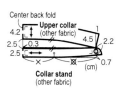

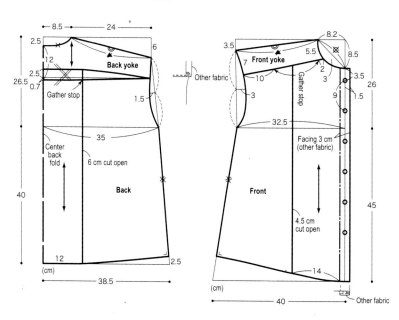

Men's shirt

Size

Bust 114 cm, Length 77.2 cm, Collar 63.5 cm

Material

Main fabric (broad stripe) … 150 cm width, 160 cm
Fusible interfacing … 90 cm width, 70 cm
Buttons … Diameter 1.2 cm, 9 pcs /
Diameter 1.1 cm, 2 pcs

Steps

*Put fusible interfacing on the back side of the left front facing,
the upper collar, the collar stand, and the cuffs.

1   Prepare the front edge. Attach the front facing to the left front
bodice (→see diagram). The right front bodice is double-folded
into a 3 cm front edge seam allowance and sewn.

2   Make and attach the pocket. →See p. 83

3   The hem seam allowance is double-folded and stitched.

4   Attach the yoke.
❶ Sandwich the back bodice with the tucks folded in between the
two yoke pieces and sew.
❷ Match the right sides of the front bodice and the outer yoke and
sew.
❸ Fold the seam allowance of the front edge of the inner yoke,
and sew up the front and back edges of the yoke.

5   Make a shirt collar with a collar stand. →See p. 53

6   Make the sleeve plackets. →See p. 64

7   Attach the sleeves with a flat-felled seam. →See p. 102

8   Sew the sleeve bottoms and the shirt sides with a flat-felled seam.

9   Attach the cuffs. →See p. 64

10   Make the buttonholes (→see p. 27) and attach the buttons.
The front edges and the cuffs use 1.3 cm buttons; the sleeve
plackets use 1.1 cm buttons.

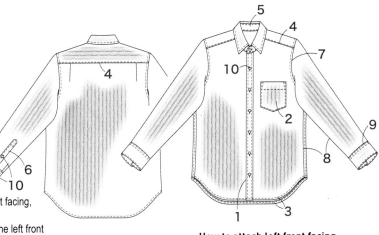

How to attach left front facing

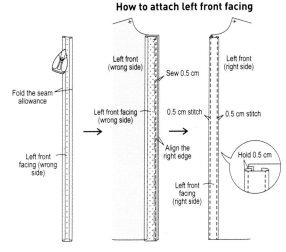

Pattern

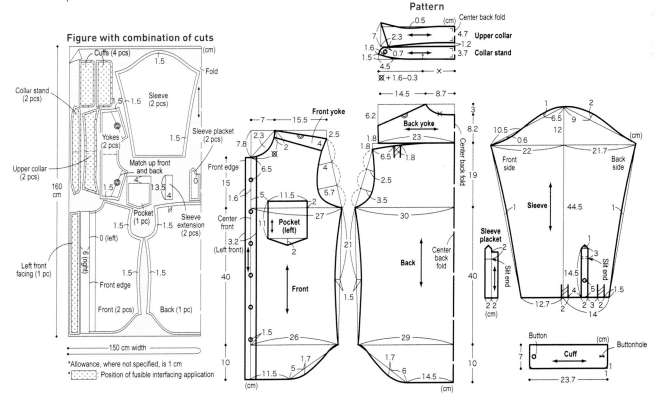

Figure with combination of cuts

Dress with rib-knit waist

Size
Bust 90cm, Waist 74 cm, Hip 94 cm, Length 92.1 cm
*Corresponding size:
Bust 80–84 cm, Waist 60–64 cm, Hip 88–92 cm

Material
Main fabric (cotton print) … 137 cm width, 120 cm
Rib-knit … 48 cm width, 20 cm
Lining (for skirt) … 90 cm width, 120 cm
Fusible interfacing … 90 cm width, 30 cm
Adhesive tape … 1.2 cm width as needed
Metal zipper … 3 cm width, 53 cm, 1 pc

Steps
*Put fusible interfacing on the back and front of the neckline and the back hem slit facing, and adhesive tape on the neckline seam allowance.
*Overcast stitch (or zigzag stitch) the seam allowance of the center back, shoulders, sides, hems, armholes, and outer edge of the facings, and the sides and center back of the rib-knit.

1 Sew darts in the bodice and skirt. Fold back seam allowance to center edge. →See p. 17

2 Sew bodice and facing shoulders, and open the seam allowance.

3 Add a facing to the neckline. →See diagram

4 Sew the bodice sides and open the seam allowance.

5 Sew the center back of the skirt, finishing above the slit.
❶ On the center back of the skirt on both right and left, fold some facing and sew a hem, then return right side out.
❷ Match the right sides of the center backs of the skirt of both right and left, sew up to the slit stop, and open the seam allowance.

6 Sew up the skirt sides and open the seam allowance.

7 Fold up and blind stitch the seam allowance on the skirt hem. Blind stitch the edge of the facing of the center back slit too.

8 Attach the rib-knit to the waist.
❶ Sew up the waist rib-knit sides and open the seam allowance.
❷ Match the right sides of the bodice waist and the rib-knit, stretch the rib-knit and sew, and overcast stitch on the seam allowance. →See p. 116
❸ Sew together the rib-knit lower edge and the skirt waist as in ❷.

9 Attach the zipper to the center back. Finish off the neckline. →See diagram

10 Make the sleeves. Fold up and sew the armhole allowance, creating a gathering in the sleeve cap.

11 Attach the sleeves. Finish off both sleeves on the seam allowance with overcast stitching. Sew back the bias fabric from the armhole below the sleeve attachment stop in order to finish off. →See p. 35

12 Sew together the lining. →See diagram

13 Attach the lining.
❶ Match the wrong sides of the skirt and the lining, and blind stitch the center back zipper crotch and slit crotch.
❷ Fold up the waist seam allowance on the lining, and where the rib-knit attachment seam is, stretch and blind stitch the rib-knit.

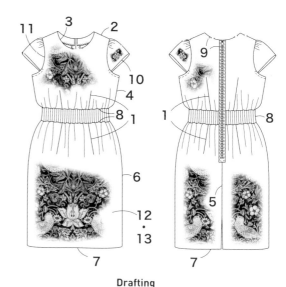

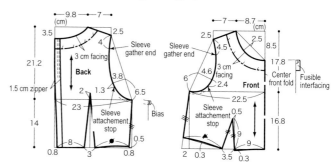

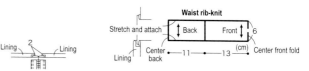

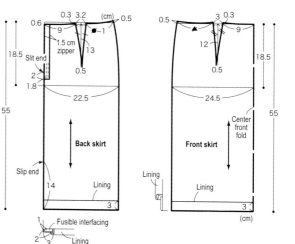

3 Add facing to the neckline

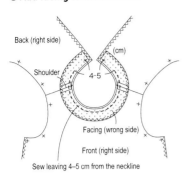

- Back (right side)
- (cm)
- Shoulder
- 4–5
- Facing (wrong side)
- Front (right side)
- Sew leaving 4–5 cm from the neckline

9 Attach the zipper to the center back, finish off the neckline

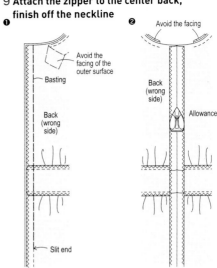

❶
- Avoid the facing of the outer surface
- Basting
- Back (wrong side)
- Slit end

❷
- Avoid the facing
- Back (wrong side)
- Allowance

12 Sew together the lining

- (Right side)
- ①
- ③ Make 1 cm cut
- ②
- Back lining (wrong side)
- ③ Make 1 cm cut
- ⑥ Sew the sides
- Front lining (right side)
- ⑥ Fold past the stitch (→p. 125)
- ⑤ Fold
- ④ Split
- ⑤ Fold
- Back lining (wrong side)
- ⑦
- 0.1
- 1.5
- Double-fold 1.5 cm
- (cm)

❸
- Avoid seam allowance
- 0.4
- Back (right side)
- Zipper (right side)
- Stitch avoiding seam allowance
- Slit end
- Fold
- 1–1.5
- (cm)
- Avoid seam allowance
- 0.4
- Back (right side)
- Zipper (right side)
- Stitch avoiding seam allowance
- (cm)

❹
- Fold back 0.5 cm
- Zipper
- Facing (wrong side)
- Center back
- Back (right side)
- Overlap 2–3 cm
- Facing (wrong side)
- Center back
- Back (right side)

❺
- Cut seam allowance 0.5 cm
- Back (right side)
- Facing (right side)
- Blind stitch
- Back (wrong side)

❻
- Back (right side)
- Stitch in zipper end
- 0.1
- (cm)

Figure with combination of cuts

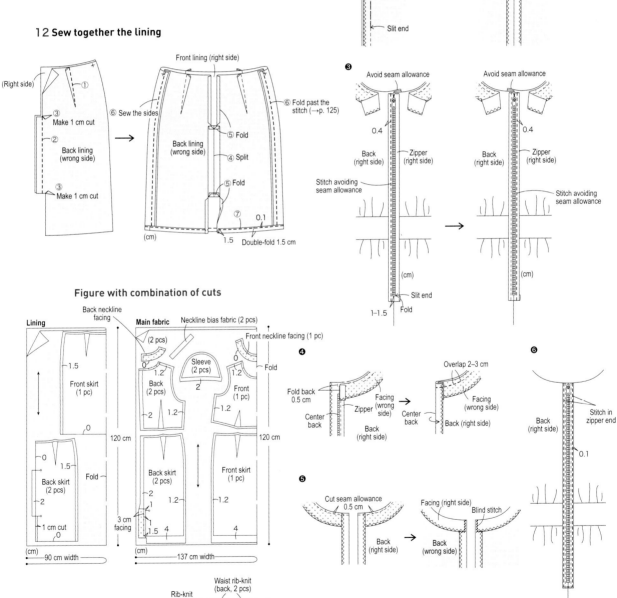

Lining
- Back neckline facing
- 1.5
- Front skirt (1 pc)
- 0
- 0
- 1.5
- Fold
- Back skirt (2 pcs)
- 2
- 1 cm cut
- 0
- 120 cm
- (cm)
- 90 cm width

Main fabric
- Neckline bias fabric (2 pcs)
- (2 pcs)
- Front neckline facing (1 pc)
- Sleeve (2 pcs)
- Fold
- 0
- 1.2
- 0
- 1.2
- Back (2 pcs)
- 2
- Front (1 pc)
- 2
- 1.2
- 120 cm
- Back skirt (2 pcs)
- 2
- 1
- 1.2
- Front skirt (1 pc)
- 1.2
- 3 cm facing
- 1.5
- 4
- 4
- (cm)
- 137 cm width

Rib-knit
- Waist rib-knit (back, 2 pcs)
- Rib-knit
- (Front, 1 pc)
- 20 cm
- 48 cm width

*Allowance, where not specified, is 1 cm

* [illustration] : Position of fusible interfacing/tape application

Jumper with pleated skirt

Size
Bust 98 cm, Waist 100 cm, Hip 100 cm, Length 85 cm
*Corresponding size:
Bust 82–86 cm, Hip 92–96 cm

Material
Main fabric (undyed taffeta) … 137 cm width, 310 cm
Lining … 90 cm width, 250 cm
Fusible interfacing … 90 cm width, 35 cm
Adhesive tape … 1.2 cm width as needed

Cutting points
Outer skirt is cut to 75 x 100 cm (length including pleats),
including a lengthways seam allowance, and the exterior fold
and shadow fold pleats are marked with the dimensions on
the figure on p. 123.
Make a paper template for the lining to the dimensions
indicated on the figure on p. 123.

Steps
*Put fusible interfacing on the wrong side of each facing,
and adhesive tape on the wrong side of the neckline seam
allowance of the main fabric.
*Overcast stitch (or zigzag stitch) the hem seam allowance of
the outer skirt.

1 Add lining to the bodice.
   ❶ Roughly stitch the seam allowance matching the wrong
   sides of both the lining and the main fabric for both the
   front and back bodice.
   ❷ In the shoulder and the side seam allowances, overcast
   stitch both parts together.
2 Sew up the shoulders and open the seam allowance.
3 Sew up the neckline. →See diagram
4 Sew up the bodice and open the seam allowance.
5 Sew back a facing on the armholes same as the neckline.
6 Fold up and stitch the seam allowance on the skirt hem.
7 Fold pleats into the skirt, and sew the sides. →See p. 108
8 Sew up the skirt lining. →See diagram
9 Sew up the waist.
   ❶ Match the wrong sides of the skirt and the lining, and
   sew the waist seam allowance.
   ❷ Match the right sides of the bodice and the skirt waist,
   and sew.
   ❸ Overcast stitch the seam allowances of all four parts at
   once, and fold back toward the bodice side.

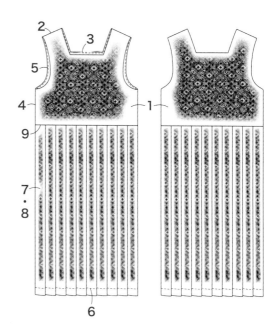

Drafting

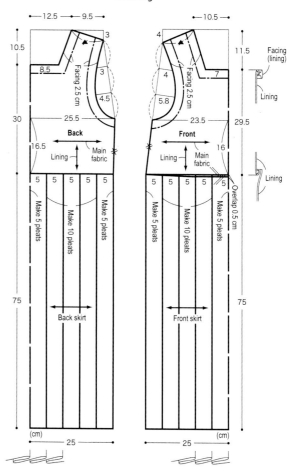

3 Sew up the neckline

❶

Back neckline facing (wrong side)

Fold seam allowance

Front neckline facing (wrong side)

❷ Sew shoulder

Back neckline facing (right side)

Front neckline facing (wrong side)

❸

Facing (wrong side)

Back (right side)

Cut in the corners

Front (right side)

❹

Back (lining)

Facing (right side)

② Turn the facing to the right side and smooth with an iron

③ Blind stitch

Front (lining)

0.1

Front (right side)

① Lapped seam on the facing and seam allowance

8 Sew up the lining

① Fold a tuck and sew

③ Overcast stitching

Lining (wrong side)

0.5 cm fold past the stitch (→p. 125)

② Sew the sides

Slit end

Double-fold 0.8 cm

④ Double-fold the slit and sew it up

Double-fold 1 cm

⑤ Double-fold the hem allowance and sew

Figure with combination of cuts

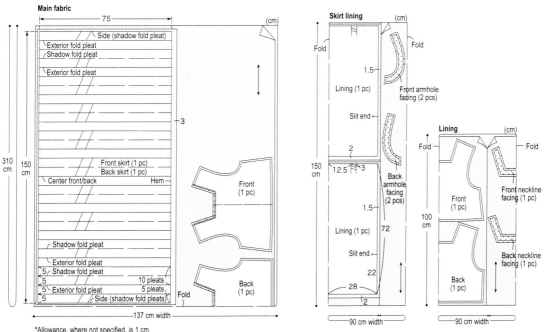

Main fabric

75

(cm)

Side (shadow fold pleat)
Exterior fold pleat
Shadow fold pleat
Exterior fold pleat

3

Front skirt (1 pc)
Back skirt (1 pc)
Center front/back   Hem

Front (1 pc)

Shadow fold pleat
Exterior fold pleat
5 Shadow fold pleat
5   10 pleats
5 Exterior fold pleat 5 pleats
5 Side (shadow fold pleats)

Back (1 pc)

Fold

310 cm   150 cm

137 cm width

Skirt lining   (cm)

Fold

1.5

Lining (1 pc)

Slit end

2

12.5 3

1.5

Lining (1 pc)

Slit end

72

22

28

2

Fold

Front armhole facing (2 pcs)

Back armhole facing (2 pcs)

150 cm

90 cm width

Lining   (cm)

Fold

Front (1 pc)

Back (1 pc)

Fold

Front neckline facing (1 pc)

Back neckline facing (1 pc)

100 cm

90 cm width

*Allowance, where not specified, is 1 cm

* [⠿⠿] : Position of fusible interfacing/tape application

Pants

Size

Waist 79 cm, Hip 101 cm, Length (center front length) 86 cm
*Corresponding size:
Waist 66–70 cm, Hip 90–95 cm

Material

Main fabric (middle stripe) … 148 cm width, 150 cm
Lining … 90 cm width, 140 cm
Sleek linig … 102 cm width, 50 cm
Fusible interfacing … 90 cm width, 60 cm
Buttons … Diameter 1.8 cm, 10 pcs / 1.5 cm, 2 pcs

Steps

*Put fusible interfacing on the wrong sides of the front and back
waist facing, the front fly facing, the fly guard, each hem panel
outer part, the piping, and the belt loop A.
*Overcast stitch (or zigzag stitch) the sides and the panel seam
of the pants, and the inseam and the panel seam of the inseam
panels, both front and back.

1 Sew darts in the back pants and fold the seam allowance on the
center side. →See p. 17

2 Form a piping pocket in the back pants. →See p. 94

3 Form a side pocket on the front pants. – ›See diagram

4 Sew together all front and back pants and front and back
inseam panels. Open the seam allowance.

5 Sew the crotch line. In front sew from the slit end downward, in
back sew from the waist side ending point downward.

6 Sew the sides and open the seam allowance.

7 Continue sewing the right and left inseams, and open the seam
allowance.

8 Sew the hem panels together. →See diagram

9 Sew the lining together.
❶ Sew the crotch line. Sew from 0.5 cm below the slit end down
to the inseam.
❷ Sew the sides, adding fullness. →See diagram
❸ Continue sewing the left and right inseam, adding fullness.
❹ Double-fold and stitch a hem seam allowance.
❺ Match the center back and the sides of the waist facing and
sew. Open the seam allowance. Sew the center back from the
ending point downward.
❻ Sew together the waist facing and ❹.

10 Match the lining and outer pants and form a front fly, sew
back the waist. →See p. 79

11 Form a belt loop.
❶ Sew back belt loop A double and fasten to the center
back.
❷ For belt loop B, fold the 2.5 x 30 cm fabric wrong side out
and sew at 1 cm width. Return right side out, cut into four
parts and sew it into position.

12 Attach the buttons. 1.8 cm diameter buttons on the front fly
and the hems, 1.5 cm buttons on the back piping pockets.

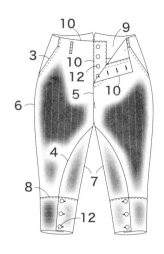

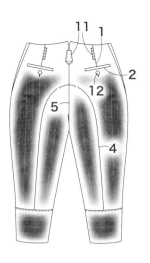

Drafting

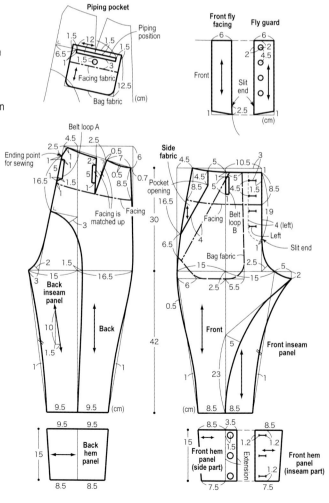

3 Form a side pocket on the front pants

8 Sew the hem panels together

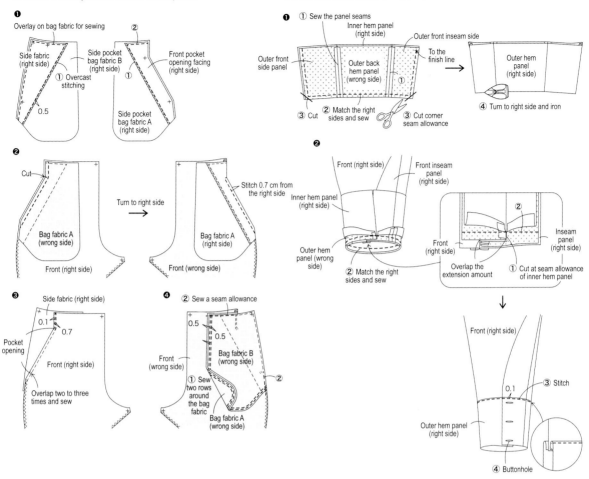

❶ Overlay on bag fabric for sewing

Side fabric (right side)
Side pocket bag fabric B (right side)
Front pocket opening facing (right side)
① Overcast stitching
0.5
Side pocket bag fabric A (right side)

❷ Cut
Bag fabric A (wrong side)
Front (right side)
Turn to right side
Stitch 0.7 cm from the right side
Bag fabric A (right side)
Front (wrong side)

❸ Side fabric (right side)
0.1
0.7
Pocket opening
Front (right side)
Overlap two to three times and sew

❹ ② Sew a seam allowance
0.5
0.5
Front (wrong side)
Bag fabric B (wrong side)
① Sew two rows around the bag fabric
②
Bag fabric A (wrong side)

❶ ① Sew the panel seams
Inner hem panel (right side)
Outer front inseam side
Outer front side panel
Outer back hem panel (wrong side)
To the finish line
①
② Match the right sides and sew
③ Cut
③ Cut corner seam allowance
Outer hem panel (right side)
④ Turn to right side and iron

❷ Front (right side)
Front inseam panel (right side)
Inner hem panel (right side)
②
Outer hem panel (wrong side)
② Match the right sides and sew
Front (right side)
Overlap the extension amount
Inseam panel (right side)
① Cut at seam allowance of inner hem panel

Front (right side)
0.1
③ Stitch
Outer hem panel (right side)
④ Buttonhole

Figure with combination of cuts

Main fabric
Front hem panel inseam side (4 pcs)
Back hem panel (4 pcs)
(cm)
Outer extension (2 pcs)
Outer side
Outer side
Front hem panel side part (4 pcs)
Front crotch facing (1 pc)
Outer side
Pocket opening facing (2 pcs)
Front waist facing (2 pcs)
Side fabric (2 pcs)
Front inseam panel (2 pcs)
Back waist facing (2 pcs)
Front (2 pcs)
Back (2 pcs)
Belt loop B (4 pcs in one)
Back inseam panel
Belt loop A (2 pcs)
Piping fabric (2 pcs)
7
30
15
2.5
0.7
150 cm
Piping pocket facing (2 pcs)
148 cm width

Lining
(cm)
Fold
Back (2 pcs)
1.5
1.5
2
Front (2 pcs)
1.5
1.5
2
Fold
140 cm
90 cm width

9 Add fullness to the lining

Wrong sides
Finish line
Sewing
Lining (wrong side)
0.2–0.5 cm (fullness)
(Wrong side)
Fold at the finish line
(Wrong side)
Fullness
Fold to one side
(Wrong side)

Sleek lining
Inner extension (1 pc)
Piping pocket bag fabric (4 pcs)
Fold
Side pocket bag fabric A (2 pcs)
Side pocket bag fabric B (2 pcs)
50 cm
102 cm width

*Allowance, where not specified, is 1 cm

* [dotted]: Position of fusible interfacing/tape application

Asymmetric skirt

Size

Waist 74 cm, Hip 102 cm, Skirt length 65–88 cm
*Corresponding size:
Waist 66–72 cm, Hip 90–100 cm

Material

Main fabric (wool tartan check) … 150 cm width, 150 cm
Fusible interfacing … 90 cm width, 15 cm
Adhesive tape … 1.2 cm width as needed
Concealed zipper … 22 cm, 1 pc

Steps

*Put fusible interfacing on the wrong side of the front and
back waist facings.
*Apply adhesive tape to the wrong side of the right
front, right back, left front, and left back skirt waist seam
allowance.
*Overcast stitch (or zigzag stitch) to the right front, right
back, left front, and left back skirt side seam allowance.
1 Put a staystitch in all parts' hems.
2 Sew in the darts, putting the seam allowance into the
center. →See p. 17
3 Sew the right back and right front sides of the skirt, and
open a seam allowance.
4 Sew the center back hem flare and right back hem flare
together (for the upper edge stop sewing at the finish
line), and sew the right back hem flare and right front
hem flare together.
5 Sew 3 and 4 together. →See diagram
6 Sew the left side. →See diagram
7 Sew 6 and the left front hem flare together.
→See diagram
8 Attach concealed zipper to the left side. →See p. 67

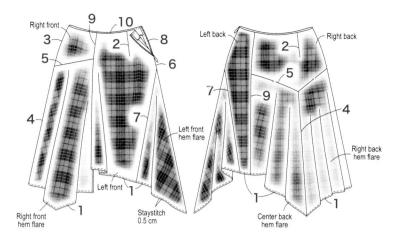

9 Sew 5 and 8 together.
  ❶ Match the right sides of 5 and 8 and sew both sides.
  ❷ Overlock stitch the two seam allowances together and put them into
  the center.
10 Sew back at the waist facing.
  ❶ Sew up the right side of both front and back waist facings,
  open the seam allowance.
  ❷ Match the right sides of the facing and the skirt waist, sew and
  open the seam allowance. Fold the left side 0.5 cm short of the edge
  of the facing end toward the wrong side, then sew the waist with the
  zipper attached seam allowance folded toward the right side so as to
  sandwich the facing.
  ❸ With the waist seam allowance folded into the facing side, sew it
  up with the overlapped seam on the facing and seam allowance.
  ❹ Return the facing to the wrong side of the skirt and straighten with
  an iron.
  ❺ Blind stitch the left side waist facing.

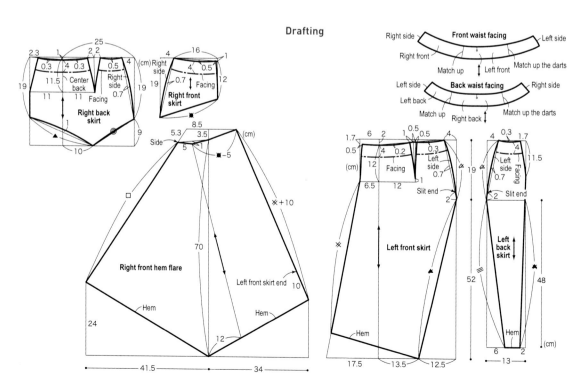

5 Sew 3 and 4 together

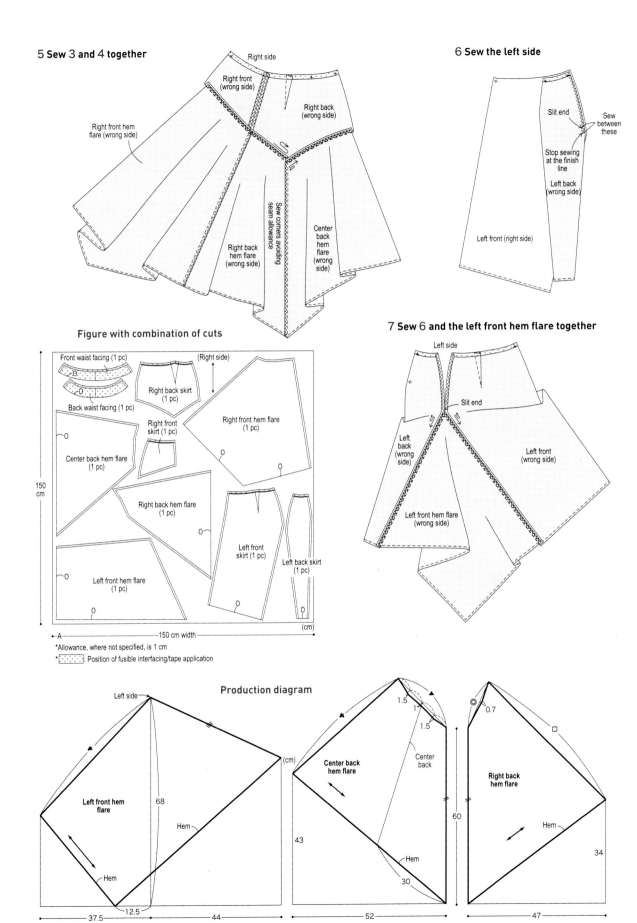

Right side

Right front
(wrong side)

Right back
(wrong side)

Right front hem
flare (wrong side)

Sew corners avoiding
seam allowance

Right back
hem flare
(wrong side)

Center
back
hem
flare
(wrong
side)

6 Sew the left side

Slit end

Sew
between
these

Stop sewing
at the finish
line

Left back
(wrong side)

Left front (right side)

Figure with combination of cuts

Front waist facing (1 pc)

(Right side)

Right back skirt
(1 pc)

Back waist facing (1 pc)

Right front hem flare
(1 pc)

Right front
skirt (1 pc)

150
cm

Center back hem flare
(1 pc)

Right back hem flare
(1 pc)

Left front
skirt (1 pc)

Left back skirt
(1 pc)

Left front hem flare
(1 pc)

(cm)

A — 150 cm width —

*Allowance, where not specified, is 1 cm

* [:::::::] : Position of fusible interfacing/tape application

7 Sew 6 and the left front hem flare together

Left side

Slit end

Left
back
(wrong
side)

Left front
(wrong side)

Left front hem flare
(wrong side)

Production diagram

Left side

Left front hem
flare

68

Hem

Hem

37.5   12.5   44

(cm)

1.5
1
1.5

Center back
hem flare

Center
back

Left back
(wrong
side)

43

Hem

30

52

0.7

Right back
hem flare

60

Hem

34

47

127

Naoko Domeki is a freelance writer specializing in dressmaking and sewing. She is highly acclaimed for her pattern drawings and easy-to-follow explanations.

Shihoko Makino is a freelance couturier and involved in a variety of projects from Paris collections to clothing in ads and more.

Publisher of Japanese Edition: Sunao Onuma

Book Design: Maiko Yoshino

Photography: Josui Yasuda (BUNKA PUBLISHING BUREAU)

Digital Trace: BUNKA Phototype

Proofreading: Masako Mukai

Editor: Nobuko Hirayama (BUNKA PUBLISHING BUREAU)

English Translation and Proofreading: TRAVOD, indigo, and TIME & SPACE, INC.

Learn Skills to Sew like a Professional
by Naoko Domeki, Shihoko Makino

English edition published in 2019 by:

NIPPAN IPS Co., Ltd.

1-3-4 Yushima

Bunkyo-ku Tokyo

113-0034 Japan

Kirei na Shitate no Puro no Waza

Copyright © Naoko Domeki, Shihoko Makino 2016

Original Japanese edition is published by EDUCATIONAL FOUNDATION BUNKA GAKUEN BUNKA PUBLISHING BUREAU

ISBN 978-4-86505-078-3

Printed in China